MOOD INDIGO

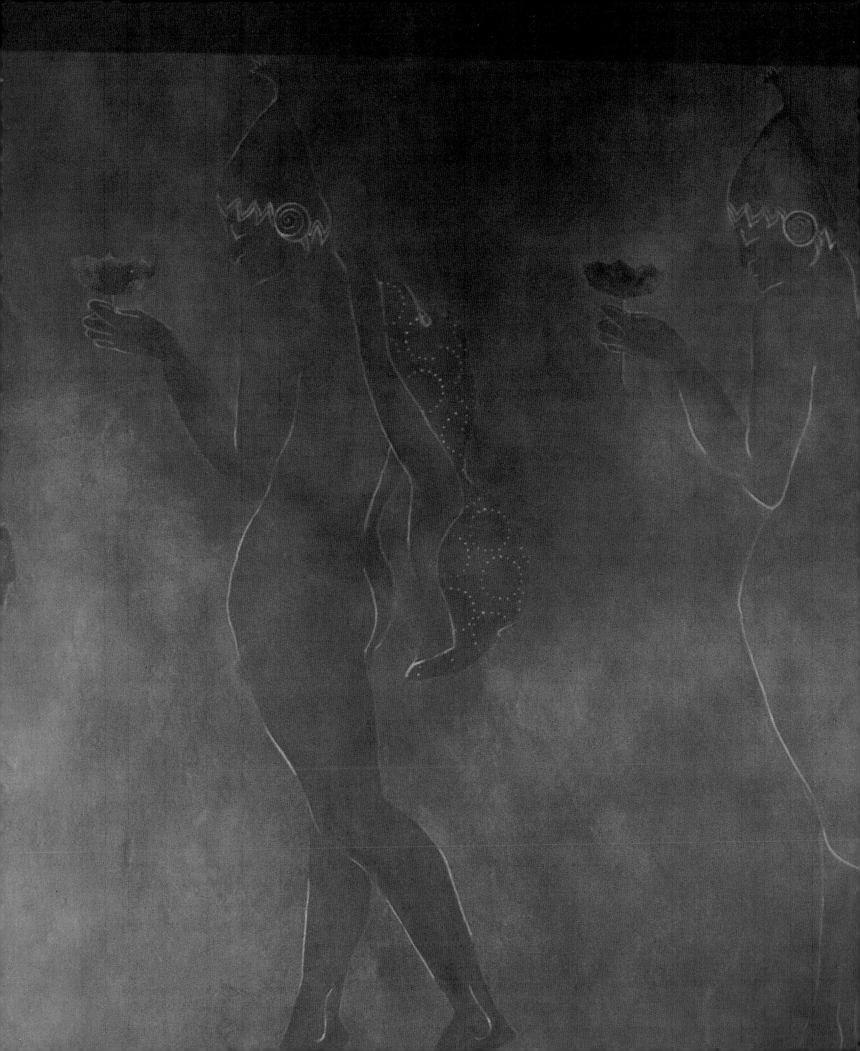

MOOD INDIGO

Vinny Lee

WATSON-GUPTILL PUBLICATIONS/NEW YORK

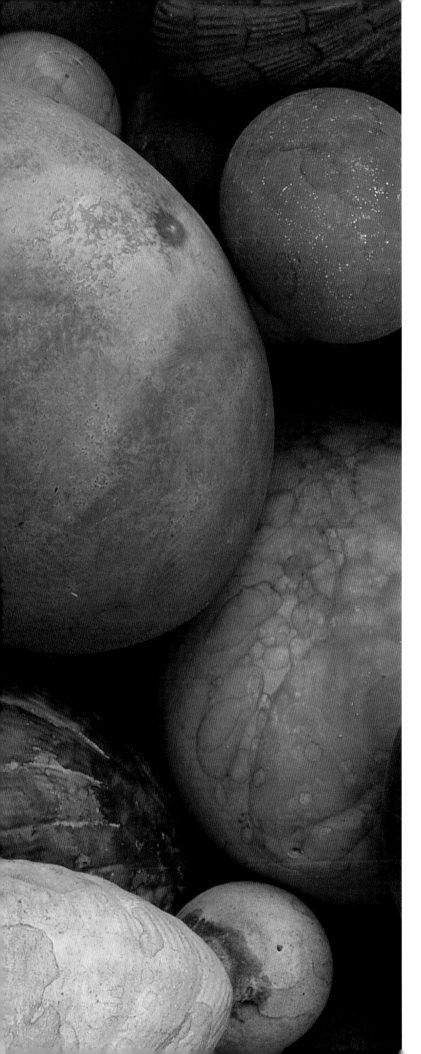

To AWJ, always my favorite color

Text © Vinny Lee 2001
Design and layout © Pavilion Books Ltd.

First published in the United States in 2001 by
Watson-Guptill Publications
a division of BPI Communications, Inc.,
770 Broadway, New York, NY 10003
www.watsonguptill.com

Designed by Helen Lewis
Text set in 9-pt Palatino Light

Library of Congress Catalog Card Number: 00–108526

ISBN 0-8230-3136-5

First published in the United Kingdom in 2001 by
Pavilion Books, Limited
London House, Great Eastern Wharf
Parkgate Road, London SW11 4NQ

Printed in Singapore by Imago
Originated by Colourpath, London

First printing, 2001

1 2 3 4 5 6 7 8 / 08 07 06 05 04 03 02 01

CONTENTS

INTRODUCTION

Color, especially rich tones, will create a statement in any room, and will establish an atmosphere and mood that will in turn affect the way you feel. The Victorian artist and critic John Ruskin said "The purest and most thoughtful minds are those which love color the most."

If you think of color in musical terms, dark tones are like the bass notes in a composition. They contribute a grounding influence to a scheme and create a balance against which light and bright notes will sound or appear all the more brilliant.

When learning a new piece of music on the piano you usually start by picking out the tune or melody with the right hand, but the piece becomes whole when the bass or left hand is added. Imagine a great piece of music, whether jazz or classical, being played with only the upper range of notes. It would lose a large part of its character and harmony—and the same can be said in decorating terms. The bass, or darker, end of the color spectrum provides shades that add authority and quickly establish a mood, which the blank canvas of white or pale-colored walls often fails to do.

For those new to decorating and living with dark colors, there are several misunderstandings and misconceptions that need to be clarified. First, dark colors don't have to be overpowering or somber—they can be inviting and comforting. Secondly, rich colors aren't the exclusive domain of wealthy and opulent dwellings, although deep-colored walls do provide a splendid setting against which gilded or silvered frames, glass, and mirrors look attractive. Dark-colored walls can be equally successful in minimalist schemes, as the color itself will be a dominant feature and will create interest as well as establish an ambience.

Thirdly, the general guideline that on walls and surfaces dark colors advance and pale colors recede is true, but much depends on the shape and style of the room, the finish applied to the walls, and the arrangement of lights and furniture. In fact, the opposite may be realized: Dark colors can be used to disguise and camouflage ugly or intrusive features. The dark color will make them appear to recede into the background while the eye is attracted to lighter or more ornate aspects of the room.

Finally, there is the fashionable element. Is a dark color going to date quickly and is this the right time to make a change from a pale scheme? Fashions and trends in interiors move quickly, but fashions are just that: fashions. And in the circular progress of things, after every period of pale and austere surroundings there comes an antidote: the return of color.

LIVING WITH STRONG COLOR

Color is a very personal thing. There are always people who disregard voguish trends and follow their instincts or alternative agendas, so although not always obvious, dark colors can be perennial. The interiors of the great and classic houses are known for staying with schemes and designs that suit the style of building and please their owners, rather than being ever-changing kaleidoscopes of modish statements.

You should, above all, choose shades that make you and your family feel comfortable. A color that one person may find warming may, to you, be overpowering; a shade that to you is relaxing may come across as cold to someone else—when choosing colors, it comes down to the individual.

Many people are wary of strong colors and of making such an assured statement when decorating their homes, but the effect can be dramatic and rewarding. If you have been used to living with white or only the hints of colors, it may take time for your eyes to get accustomed to rich, dark shades, but it is worth trying.

Because the background in this room is dark, the elegant classic chair with white velvet upholstery and silver printing stands out. The eye is drawn to the chair's detail and finish, including the silvered polish on its carved wood.

ABOVE: *This exotic bedroom-cum-library is decorated with gold trims and frames that add to its decadent appearance. A large mirror reflects both natural and artificial light, making the room less oppressive.*

LEFT: *Historically, rich colors have been used to add warmth to large, cold rooms and to bring a feeling of comfort and intimacy. In this traditionally furnished sitting room, the colors not only fulfill that goal but also complement the furnishings and accessories.*

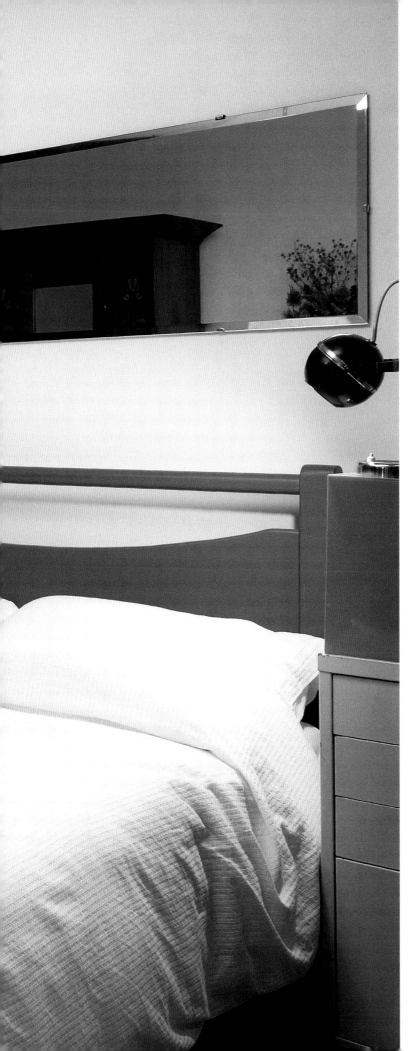

It can also take time and courage to build up the impetus to put strong color on your walls. Try taking it step by step. Paint one wall a deep color and live with it for a few weeks until you get used to it. Or start with an undercoat of a paler shade and add a top layer of the darker color later, so you have time to adapt and become familiar with the change. It is always easier to start lighter and go darker than to start dark and go light, as it may take several coats of a paler color to obliterate the darker one.

Also, remember that when you first see bare walls painted in a dark color they may appear very strong and even overwhelming. But as soon as you put carpets, furniture, pictures, lights, and soft furnishings into the room, the amount of visible, dark space will be dramatically reduced.

COLOR AND TEXTURE

The type of finish you choose for your walls will also influence the overall effect. A matte, chalky surface will make a dark tone seem duskier and soft, even silky, whereas a rich gloss will exaggerate the richness, hardness, and depth of color. Soft finishes include the standard modern matte and silk paints, although silk does have a muted sheen. Traditional patinas include distemper and limewash.

Distemper is a chalk-based finish with a powdery quality. Historically, the problem with distemper has been that it has a tendency to rub off if a person or furniture brushes against it, leaving a white or dusty mark on clothes or upholstery. It was also unsuitable for washing, as the chalk content made it absorb water and any liquid stains, wax, or grease marks. Nowadays,

In this contemporary bedroom, dark furniture is used to bring gravitas to a neutral scheme. The hallway, decorated in a hot, strong orange, acts as a foil to the monochromatic bedroom, offering a warm passageway after the bedroom's coolness.

ABOVE: *Delicate coral, shells, and dried leaves are accentuated by dark surroundings. The intricacies of their veins and branches can be seen in detail when placed against a black or black-based color.*

RIGHT: *Deep blues and reds work well together. These dark blue walls create a solid background for the red velvet sofas and gray marble fireplace. A light-colored ceiling and floor prevent the room from feeling oppressive or claustrophobic.*

LEFT: Gold and gilt frames, shelves, and pictures add to the richness of this room; the painted wood floor and dark-chocolate framed daybed help to balance the heat of the rich terra-cotta wall color. Accessories, such as the cushion, combine the two main colors and bring the whole scheme together.

ready-made, washable distempers are available from specialist paint and decorating shops and they can be used successfully to create the soft, antique finish that gives walls a period appearance.

Limewash was traditionally used as a way of brightening and usually whitening the outsides of houses, cottages, and rural buildings, and is still used in some countries. Limewash can be colored with pigments and is sometimes used indoors to create a country style, as it is slightly mottled and has a worn look on walls. The lime element can be corrosive when wet, so protective clothing and eyewear is advisable when working with it.

As paint manufacturers become increasingly technologically advanced, metallic finishes are also growing in popularity—mainly because they are becoming less expensive and much easier to apply in domestic settings. Metallic paints can be highly effective on walls in dimly lit areas, such as windowless corridors, dining rooms (which may be lit by candlelight), and even an indulgent bathroom, where lights may be dimmed to a subtle level for a relaxing soak. Under soft electric lights or candlelight the metallic particles in the paint will appear to glitter, creating a magical and unusual environment.

For a harder, shiny finish, there is the modern full-gloss paint. But be careful when choosing your gloss paint as some are designed for external use only. Others are specifically formulated for internal walls and should be applied over a base coat and well-prepared wall. If you are hoping to achieve a lacquerlike finish, the wall surface must be immaculate before you apply the paint, otherwise any flecks of dust or stray hairs from a brush will create an unsightly blemish.

ABOVE: Even on rustic walls, such as this rough-hewn timber, red-based colors give warmth and a feeling of comfort. Many buildings of the Shaker community in New England are painted a rich, deep red; it is also a color associated with rural barns and buildings.

Fabric, whether a plain cotton, slub silk, or an integral woven jacquard pattern, stripe, or other design, will create yet another effect. Fabric dampens noise in a room and can add to the feeling of luxury and wealth, although it may make a small room seem even smaller.

Fabric can be used in many ways. For example, it may be battened tight against the wall so that it looks like wallpaper. It can also be draped and tented, transforming a small boxy room into an exotic Bedouin- or safari-style tent space. Fabric may also be attached to panels and applied onto painted walls, which lends an appearance of period-style elegance.

For those wanting something with a historic feel, or even an oriental lacquer effect, a plain matte base paint can be given a gloss finish by covering it with layers of transparent glaze, which will intensify the color and add a glasslike sheen. A number of glazes are available, including crackle glaze, which dries to a cracked, ancient appearance, like old pottery.

Lacquers were originally made from tree resin, but now there are modern versions that give the same high-gloss finish seen on oriental furniture and *objets d'art*. On furniture and smaller surface areas, the high sheen is traditionally built up with repeated applications of the lacquer; each layer is sanded down when dry and then covered with another coat, until several layers of the varnish are produced and the final layer achieves an immaculate, glassy finish. Today, modern varnishes and high-gloss paints can create the same effect in a fraction of the time and with considerably less effort.

Glazed ceramic tile is another surface that suits deep and rich colorings. Bottle or pine green tiles can be attractive in a conservatory; rich blue may suit a country or Mediterranean-style kitchen-cum-dining room.

ABOVE: *Instead of a solid black floor, a grid arrangement of ceramic tiles has been used. The configuration of tiles and white joins creates an interesting geometric design, and the white grout reduces the denseness of the black without diminishing its impact.*

A row of dark-colored tiles behind a modern steel kitchen countertop or sink can create a striking contrast to the shiny hardness of the metal. Dark tile borders will also stand out well against standard white sanitary units and baths, and will make a shower enclosure a more interesting feature in the corner of an otherwise plain bathroom.

COLOR AND LIGHT

Lighting is a very important feature in dark-colored rooms. Its arrangement and strength determines how functional a space is, and affects the strength of color in the room.

Dark colors react very differently to natural and artificial light. In winter daylight these colors look deeper, and in most cases somewhat flat, so well-placed artificial light is required to help lift the ambience. The actual surface finish of the wall also plays an important role in the overall lighting scheme. Glossy and metallic finishes reflect a certain amount of light, making the space seem larger; matte and fabric surfaces tend to absorb light, so stronger bulbs or more lamps may be necessary.

Ambient lighting—the basic, overall lighting in a room—can be a mix of wall lights (which, when in attractive shades, will become features against the dark walls) and a central light. The central light may only be required at certain times, as direct overhead lighting can be wearing on the eyes, but it is very useful on first entering a room and taking an overview of the space.

LEFT: *This bold blue wall will look different in various types of lighting. The natural daylight through the door is a white light that makes the blue appear slightly paler and less intense. But at night, when bedside lights are lit, the color will appear darker and deeper.*

OVERLEAF LEFT: *The sensual textures of velvet, fake fur, and suede in shades of coffee, toffee, and milk chocolate are rich but not overpowering, and can be used to furnish and lighten a room painted in a deep shade, such as cocoa brown.*

OVERLEAF RIGHT: *The walls in this bedroom have been finished with a dark brown matte paint, against which the tea-colored bed linens and curtains appear antique and delicate. A large, silky, off-white fake fur throw and cushion stand out against the deeper shades and create a feeling of decadence and style.*

Floor-level lighting fixtures placed in the corners of a room will direct columns of light upward and give an exaggerated feeling of height, which can be an asset if you have a dark-colored ceiling as well. Free-standing floor lamps can be used for the same effect, although because of their stands they will become part of the furnishing as well as the lighting scheme, and the light will be projected from a starting point farther up the wall, leaving the area underneath the light in shadow.

Task lighting, such as adjustable reading lights, should be placed by chairs so that the occupants can have sufficient, readily available illumination for close work or newspaper browsing. Decorative lights can be used to highlight features, such as colored glass bowls, a piece of sculpture, or an ornate gilded frame and painting.

To make the most of the many moods and uses of a room, adjustable lighting on dimmer switches is useful. You can also have a variety of lights connected to one circuit that, with the flick of a switch, will turn on all the ambient wall lights to give a basic overall light to the room. You might then put the decorative lighting on a separate circuit so that for a dark, moody atmosphere you can have just the decorative lighting with candles, and for a more welcoming, general setting the two levels can be used together.

LET THE DAYLIGHT IN

If the windows of a richly decorated room are small, it is best not to clutter them with heavy or oversized curtains and dressings. To make the most of available light, paint the frames of the window (and, if set into the wall, the panels on either side) in a pale, white-based reflective color so that the available natural light is amplified rather than absorbed.

A reflective surface, such as a mirror, on the wall opposite the window will also help double the effect of the available light. In a bedroom or dressing room, a wall of built-in wardrobes with mirrored doors will not only be useful for checking your appearance, but will also give the feeling of added space and light.

Curtain treatments should be kept simple and well tied back or draped around corbels away from the edge of the window. It is important to have a good flow of natural light in a dark room, otherwise it can feel oppressive.

LOOK TO THE PAST

When starting on a scheme employing rich colors, it can be inspiring and informative to take a look back at periods of history when dark colors were used. One of the most notable early periods of luxuriant color was between the fourteenth and sixteenth centuries in the homes of the nobility in France, Italy, and England.

During this time the homes of the wealthy were large and cool. This was comparatively comfortable during the light, hot days and nights of summer, but in winter's dark days the icy drafts had to be kept at bay with thick fabrics and hangings. Intense, rich colors gave the impression of warmth and a sense of intimacy to high-ceilinged, echoing chambers, as well as a bright contrast to the dull, gray days outside.

Deep jewel colors were also a sign of wealth, as many of the colors were imported from the Far East and Orient and were expensive to produce, being laboriously extracted by drying and grinding insects and plants. Others, such as certain shades of blue, were highly prized as they were made with pigments ground down from semi-precious stones, such as lapis lazuli.

For inspiration and ideas on how to use dark and rich colors, look to the past. Many European homes, both stately and less grand, used strong color to enhance interiors and bring feelings of warmth and comfort to minimally heated rooms.

In the seventeenth century, after the term of austerity enforced under Oliver Cromwell, Restoration England embarked on a period of color and an ostentatious show of decoration. The appeal of ornamentation and color was seen yet again in Victorian England, with designers such as Pugin using Gothic motifs in reds, blues, and greens with gold to decorate buildings such as the Palace of Westminster.

The eminent Victorian author, artist, and craftsman William Morris, who rejected the clutter and artificiality of mainstream Victorian style, founded the Arts and Crafts movement in the 1800s, which extolled the virtues of nature and handmade objects. Nevertheless, he also used rich, sometimes dark colors in his own designs; many printed with pigments derived from natural sources.

The many famous buildings that make use of the power of color include, ironically, the White House, which has the oval Blue Room, where the President receives guests at state dinners, and the Red Room, where the First Lady receives her guests.

The nature of color fashion is cyclical: After recent trends focusing on minimalism, the fastidiousness of industrial design, and the pale, muted shades of Scandinavian style, a period of rich, dark color is ready to return.

Color in our surroundings is very important. Certain colors are found to invigorate while others, such as green, can be soothing and relaxing; dull, murky colors can make us feel tired and low in energy.

In hospitals and other medical institutions, it has been found that when rooms used for special purposes—such as for counseling, intensive care, and as children's wards—are decorated in certain colors, the color can play an important part in speeding up recovery. Used correctly, color can promote a feeling of well-being, encouraging a quick recovery and a positive outlook. There is more to color than, at first, meets the eye.

LEFT AND ABOVE: *In the past, intricately woven jacquard and damask fabrics were hung on walls and used as bedspreads in wealthy homes. They provided not only extra warmth but decoration as well. These figured, variegated patterned fabrics had what is now known as "tone-on-tone" decoration. Such patterns maintained the overall depth of a single color but added interest and relief over large expanses of wall. Today, wallpapers printed with similar patterns can be bought and hung at a fraction of the price of these materials.*

BLUES & GREENS

*Pale blues and greens are the fresh, cool colors of nature,
but at the other end of the spectrum they take on a new
intensity and richness.*

The family of rich blues is wide and varied, from the fresh but intense, saturated blues found in the Mediterranean to the inky, sultry midnight blues of a starlit sky, with many moods and mixes in between. Blue is a color that works well with shades from within its own family, but can also be effectively dramatic when set with a contrasting color, like an acceptable discord in a musical theme.

Dark-tone blues, such as indigo and navy, are popular in the world of fashion design. These colors are classic and timeless. Indigo-dyed denim jeans and workwear have been in use since the trading days between India and the south of France, where the name Serge de Nimes originated.

A plain, dark-blue tailored suit can be worn with a simple white shirt for an appearance of understated chic, or can be dressed up with glittering jewelery and a flash of bright color. The same applies when these deep blues are used as background colors in interior decoration; they are versatile and yet supportive to other colors.

COLOR IN HARMONY

To see what the possibilities are for color schemes based on blue, it is important to find compatible and harmonious colors that will both contrast and enhance the main shade. To do this it is helpful to consult a color wheel, like the one shown opposite. A basic color wheel comprises the same colors as the rainbow—red, orange, yellow, green, blue, indigo, and violet—but arranged in a circle instead of a line. A more elaborate wheel, like the one shown, can be devised incorporating mixed, or *tertiary,* colors in each section.

Colors on either side of your main color will be harmonious, as they have the same root color. If blue is your main color, harmonious colors will be green blue and purple blue. For complementary yet contrasting colors, look to the diametrically opposite side of the color wheel—for blue, that would be the yellow–orange range.

When choosing a scheme, try to include variations on the main color from within its own family—referred to in interior-design speak as "tone on tone." This can also be a good way of gradually getting used to darker schemes as you can use accessories and trimmings in pale versions of the main color to help lighten and lift the overall color of the room.

Tone on tone can be achieved in various ways. For example, a striped, hand-painted pattern or preprinted striped wallpaper of dark blue and a mid- or paler shade will create interest. The darker shade will both strengthen the paler shade and be diluted by it. It helps to try and imagine this effect in terms of light and shadow on an area of single color.

Tone on tone can also be seen in wallpapers that are printed with a self-pattern, as on a jacquard fabric. The colors of the pattern are either lighter or darker than the background color, creating texture and interest while still maintaining the overall feeling and appearance of the background color.

This same technique (of using light and dark shades of the main color) can also be applied to contrasting colors. For example, the contrasting color for blue is yellow orange, but the cushion covers, throws, and soft furnishings that you choose for a deep blue room need not all be in the exact same color. As long as the yellow tone is in there you can add orange browns and orange yellows. You may also choose to include prints or woven patterns that incorporate both the blue and variations of the contrasting colors.

As an alternative to using contrasting colors, you may wish to make a fashion statement with a bolder choice. Today, a popular partner for navy is vivid pink. By using shocking pink throws and cushions you can give the room an up-to-the-minute look. When the phase has passed, or you have grown tired of it, these accessories can easily be changed or substituted with those of another color.

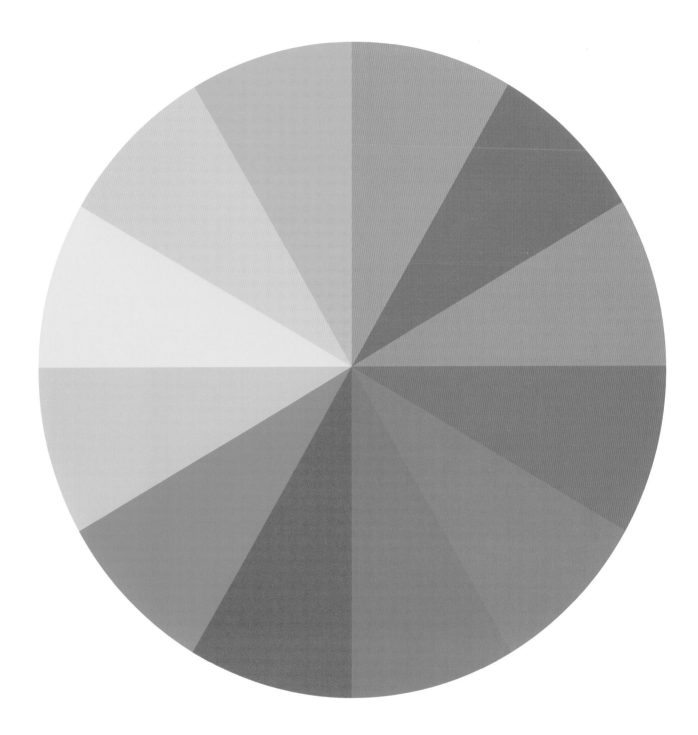

A color wheel is a helpful device for working out decorative schemes. Colors directly opposite each other, such as red and green, can be used to create a dramatic contrasting plan. Alternatively, the colors on either side of your main color, for example yellow, yellow orange, and yellow green, will create a more harmonious palette.

ABOVE: *The dark color used in the recess of this bed gives the illusion of greater depth and indicates that it is a place for nocturnal repose. Tiny stars painted on an ink black background give the impression of a night sky.*

RIGHT: *Traditional ikat fabrics in blue and white can be used as sources of inspiration for both simple and ornate schemes. Ikats can be woven in cotton for everyday use or in silk for more luxurious hangings. Many are still hand-dyed and loomed in India, especially in the region of Andhra Pradesh.*

If the walls are painted in a single strong color, then curtains, blinds, cushions, and upholstery can be places to introduce pattern. Beware, however, of creating a jumble: Try to stick to one theme, such as geometric or floral, and limit the number of colors that you introduce so you achieve a look that is cohesive.

Changing cushion covers, throws, and other soft furnishings can also be done seasonally to give the room different atmospheres. You may want warmer, cozier colors in the autumn and winter and lighter, fresher ones for the spring and summer. This can be done not only with color but with texture as well. Use rich brocades and thick velvets for the winter and coarse linens and fine cottons for the summer.

STRIKING A BALANCE

Not all walls in a room need to be the same color. Two of the walls could be painted in the main color, such as dark blue, and the other two in blue green or violet—colors with the same base note but a hint of another color. When using a scheme like this, you can then add more and more green- or red-toned accessories to swing the emphasis away from the blue toward the red or green. Following the red path, for example, you could have two walls in dark blue and two in deep plum, with colors for the accessories and curtains going from dark blackberry blue to plum, raspberry, and even lilac pink (keeping the blue note constant in the paler shades). A similar plan could be used with walls all painted the same color, by introducing the deep plum in the carpet or decoration of the ceiling.

Floors and ceilings play an important part in achieving balance and will affect the overall appearance of a room; their coloring and decoration should be taken into consideration in the early stages of planning. If you have an existing feature, such as a brick or stone floor, keep that color in mind when choosing the paint or paper for the wall. For example, with a red brick or terra-cotta tiled floor there will be a red element already in situ, so the shade of blue for the walls should also have a warm or compatible tone. If the floor is covered with greenish gray flagstones, then the blue may benefit from a hint of green gray to complement the floor finish.

Trim and baseboards can also be used to bridge the gap between walls and floors. If you have that terra-cotta floor but wish to maintain a strong blue color on the walls, then the baseboard could be painted in a warmer color to create an easier transition for the eye from the wall to the floor color.

Light wood, parquet, or plank flooring in a timber with a slightly golden hue can be used to bring a brighter element to a deep- or richly colored room, but be careful not to choose a wood that will create too leery a contrast. Wall-to-wall carpets can be a mistake, especially if they're the same color as the walls—they may make the room feel hemmed in, with no discernible edge or finish. Instead, a large rug set in the center of a paler wood floor or with a contrasting, painted edge showing, will give definition and grounding to the room.

Other features, such as doors, window frames, baseboards, or a border around a fireplace, can be painted in lighter or contrasting colors or white, which will lift and lighten the overall appearance of the room. It will also give

A range of diverse and contrasting colors can be linked in one scheme. Here, a rainbow assortment of scatter cushions brings together the main colors of the room and brightens a long, pale-colored sofa that would otherwise be in stark contrast to the deeper colors on the walls and ceiling.

ABOVE: *A warm note links the blue, purple, and copper in this recessed niche in a bathroom. Blue, a color associated with water, is popular for bathrooms.*

LEFT: *A red note links the pink, orange, and blue in this striking contemporary design. The color of the table contrasts with the deep blue panel in the foreground, yet marries with the panel on the farthest wall. Randomly placed panes of colored glass take the scheme through to the window.*

ABOVE: *Dark colors are effective in opulent schemes, as a foil to the glitter of glass, gilding, and silver. This wall of indigo blue has the effect of emphasizing the antiques and artifacts arranged in front of it, and the pair of monochromatic prints with gold frames also stands out strongly against the dark wall.*

RIGHT: *Wall surfaces can be covered in many finishes, from fabric and paint to highly glazed tiles. The type of finish will influence the depth and effect of the color. The sheen of these glazed, ink-colored tiles is highlighted by gilt detailing and a mosaic border.*

the room boundaries and points of reference. In a room with dark walls and a dark ceiling, a painted or highlighted picture rail will create a break between the walls and ceiling and prevent the ceiling from appearing low and oppressive. Similarly, if the walls are long and tall, a painted dado rail or panels will break up the expanse of single color and create a line or interruption on the continuous surface.

Existing features, such as fireplaces, should also be taken into consideration. If a tiled border around the fireplace has a floral motif with green leaves, then a wall color that is blue with a touch of yellow will be suitable, or you may choose to add a new border or paint over the existing one.

In a scheme of simple blue and white, the detailing of trims and borders can be heightened with an undercoat of dark blue or blue gray, which can then be revealed through the upper layer of white by gently sandpapering the raised edges of the motifs or carvings. For a luxurious touch, the detailing can be accentuated with a light covering of sliver leaf, either left matte or buffed to a sheen.

BLUE COLOR SCHEMES

Blue is the color that represents the sea and the sky, elements that you may wish to use for decorative schemes. For example, rooms in which water is used, such as a bathroom or kitchen, are ideal for blue-based decorations. A child's bedroom may also benefit from the calming effect of blue, perhaps in a mural of the seaside. The picture could start on one wall by depicting the morning, with people arriving at the beach, and then lead through the day and its activities to nightfall, ending on the fourth wall with a dark blue sky, silver stars, and a moon casting dappled shadows across the empty sands.

Going toward a deeper shade of blue is the blue black of midnight. This inky shade needs to be chosen and used carefully—a touch too much black, or ill-placed lighting, can make the color appear black rather than blue. Midnight blue is a sophisticated color and it looks good with silver, like the moon and stars, as well as gold, which comes from blue's complementary opposite on the color wheel (yellow orange).

Contrary to popular opinion, deep blue can even make a space seem larger. A room painted with dark blue walls and a ceiling spotted with tiny halogen lights or painted with gold stars can appear like the sky at night, as magical and as vast as infinity.

SOURCES OF INSPIRATION

For a contemporary ethnic or transglobal look, try basing a scheme around a batik or ikat fabric. *Batik* is the Javanese word for "wax painting." Designs are first painted on both sides of the cloth in melted wax; then, when the wax is set, the cloth is dipped in dye, which is absorbed by the uncovered area but resisted by the pattern covered in wax. Afterward, the wax is removed by boiling or dissolving, leaving a light pattern on a dark background. The process may be repeated many times with other colored dyes; the most frequently used colors are blue and brown.

Ikat is another ethnic pattern that is almost universal, appearing in traditional weaves from Africa, India, and Japan. The geometric base to the

There are many traditional indigo-blue-and-white cloths, varying from the intricate weaving of the ikat, found in India and Japan, to resist-dyed fabrics such as batiks and tie-dyes, for which sections of the cloth are tied tightly so that the dye does not soak through.

ABOVE: *Blue and white colors work in both traditional and modern schemes. In this more contemporary setting, blue and white mosaic tiles are bordered with white, which lessens the intensity of the dark blue element. Midtone and paler tiles have also been interspersed among the darker ones.*

LEFT: *Blue and white are a classic combination, used in homes from Scandinavia to the Mediterranean. Here, the depth of the blue—a warm shade that leans toward the red rather than green side of the color wheel—makes a strong impact.*

design makes it timeless, and it looks equally at home in a minimalist setting and a bazaar-style or fully furnished and accessorized room.

The true ikat is a woven design made of individually dyed threads. Part of the thread is dyed in one color while the other stays neutral or is dyed in a contrasting shade. The pattern is created by weaving the threads but keeping sections of the same color in place, row upon row, so that a softly edged geometric pattern, usually diamond shaped, is formed.

Although some ikat patterns are found in multicolored textiles, the purest form is the white and indigo blue combination. These colors help to concentrate the eye on the skill of the weaving and the decorative pattern in the fabric.

A blue-and-white ikat could be used as a spectacular bedspread in a simply decorated dark blue and white room, or as striking blinds on long windows. It can be incorporated into a simple Japanese theme as well as in a more multiethnic, eclectic decor.

There are also fabrics and designs that have more regal connections. Blue is often associated with holiness and royalty, and is the color of many ecclesiastical robes, including those portrayed on the Virgin Mary in statues and paintings. It is also frequently found in royal banners and as a background on shields and coats of arms. The color royal blue—a deep, pure, vivid blue—was deemed worthy of the royal prefix. Looking across a selection of the world's national flags you will see dark blue in, among many others, the Union Jack and the flags of the United States and France.

Fabrics are not the only sources of inspiration for blue schemes; numerous theme ideas can be found around the world and throughout history.

*Pale colors and directional lighting draw your eye to
the arrangement at the bottom of this stairwell. The
blue walls act as a frame to the display below, and the
columns on either side of the raised dais echo the blue of
the tunnel-like passageway.*

The Abbidad Islamic potters were among the earliest people to create tin-glazed white pots overpainted with blue decorations. This ware is believed to have inspired the blue-and-white porcelain of China, which in turn led to the rise of blue-and-white Delftware, named after the center of its manufacture when it shifted from Antwerp to Delft in the mid-seventeenth century. The name Delftware was also given to the English version made in London, Liverpool, and Bristol, as well as an Irish variant manufactured in Dublin. These well-known chinas use a rich blue for the pattern, set off against a crisp white or the palest of blue backgrounds.

These contrasting colors suit many settings, from country-style kitchens to more bourgeois sitting rooms and parlors. Perhaps the best known of all designs in this color combination is the Willow Pattern, which illustrates the tale of a lovers' tryst beneath a graceful weeping willow and oriental bridge.

From the warmer climes of the Mediterranean comes the slightly greener blue used on doors and shutters along the Greek coastline, especially in hilltop villages, which contrasts with the pristine white of the whitewashed walls. In the south of France and Provence, where lavender grows in abundance, a more purpley blue is often used on external doors and is contrasted with a pinkish terra-cotta on the walls, which adds warmth and picks up the red note in the lavender blue.

Both the artist Frida Kahlo and the fashion designer Yves St. Laurent have used this combination of vivid blue and pinkish terra-cotta in their homes. At Frida Kahlo and Diego Rivera's Blue House in Coyoacán, south of Mexico City, a vibrant blue appears in many rooms, most noticeably in the courtyard. The inner courtyard walls are solid blue, with door and window borders picked out in a rich terra-cotta red. The actual door and window frames are painted in a contrasting mint green. Around the base of the walls

ABOVE: *Practical, wipe-clean, gray-and-white flecked granite has been used as a countertop and wall covering in this kitchen, but the blue-and-white striped, tentlike ceiling and the stippled blue walls with white china add light-hearted, less formal elements to the scheme.*

LEFT: *Spectral figures in muted gold stride across an ocean of dark blue wall, creating an eye-catching feature without diminishing the power of the background color. The somber-colored furniture is in keeping with the mysterious flavor of the room.*

in most rooms is a thick band of blue, about 24 inches (60 cm) wide, while the rest of the walls are white. Sometimes a niche or recess is picked out in the same rich blue.

Fashion designer Yves St. Laurent and his business partner Pierre Berge used vivid cobalt blue when they restored the walls of the enclosed Majorelle Gardens in Marrakesh, which were originally laid out in the 1920s by French artist Jacques Majorelle. It is said that the blue was inspired by the color of the overalls worn by French workmen.

A note of warning is needed here—beware when reminiscing and dreaming of hot climes or trying to emulate or recapture the feeling of a location that you visited while on vacation, because you may be disappointed. Vivid blues may have looked wonderful in Greece, bathed in hot sunlight, but in the dark, cold winter nights of February they won't have quite the same glow.

Rich colors can, however, help lift the interior of a cold or dark home and make it cozy and comforting. Dark colors can cocoon and reassure as well as aid relaxation and form an effective barrier between the noise, traffic, and inclement weather outside.

When copying or emulating a color that you have seen in sunshine or on vacation, remember to take into consideration the negative effect of darkness and consider opting for a level or two more of intensity of color or brightness to compensate. With blue shades, a hint of a warming tone of red can help cut down on any coolness. You can also add orange and gold accessories rather than silver, pale blue, or white, which will only emphasize the cooler elements of the color.

Also remember to check colors in both natural and artificial light. For a dominant area of color, such as a wall, it is advisable to paint a generous, trial section with paint from a small sample pot. Look at the color throughout the day as the light moves and changes, and also in the evening. Try testing fabrics and other swatches against it at various times to ensure that the other colors are compatible, and that they react favorably to different levels of light.

Artificial lighting is seldom white, and the color it emits will have an effect on the surfaces on which it shines. For example, certain lighter shades of yellow will seem to be neutralized under the illumination of a standard incandescent bulb, which has a yellow tinge. Fluorescent lights, rarely used in living areas but often found in bathrooms and over kitchen counters, have a blue cast that can make a cool blue look colder. So choose the type of artificial lighting to be installed with care.

Your choice of fabrics should also be carefully considered, not just for their color and pattern but also for their texture. Deep-pile, dark-colored fabrics, such as velvet, will absorb light, as will thick wools such as felt. Reflective surface fabrics, such as satin, silk, or anything with a metallic thread, will help enhance the effect of the light.

Furniture will also be influential. Dark wood furniture, such as mahogany, will be lost against a dark navy or indigo wall unless it is carefully spotlighted or set against a panel of a paler color. Light-colored furniture, such as white-painted Scandinavian style pieces, may be too much of a contrast on their own, but if covered with cushions in a mix of blue and white fabrics will be more balanced.

In dark-colored rooms, the area around the windows should be kept clear to allow the maximum amount of daylight to enter. These classic paneled shutters have been painted so that they blend with the wall when folded back. If curtains are used they should be draped back around corbels or contained by ties.

THE SOURCES OF BLUE

The blues are a rich family of color that provide a wealth of decorating choices. Varying shades of blue can be found to suit all manner of rooms and styles, from rustic to contemporary and from traditional to high-tech.

Today, most dye stuffs tend to be synthetically manufactured, which ensures their durability and constancy, but there are still a few manufacturers who prefer to use more traditional methods and ingredients, and there are those who also add pigments to whitewash or water-based mediums to emulate a folk style or traditional finish.

Indigo, which came originally from a plant, is probably one of the best-known deep, inky blue colors. The genus Indigofera covers a family of more than 700 shrubs and herbs, and their delicate mauve, pink, and white flowers provide few clues to the rich-colored dye that their fruit pods provide. Deep hued and long lasting, this dye was used in ancient times in India, Egypt, and Rome and was introduced into Europe in the sixteenth century.

Woad, a plant from the mustard family, was also used to produce a blue dye, favored not just for cloth dying but also as a war paint worn on the skin. Boudicca, the warrior queen of the Iceni, and her troops who fought against the Romans in AD 43 wore the dye.

Prussian blue is a chemical colorant that was initially formed from ferrous and ferric ions combined with cyanide and cyanide compounds and was introduced in the early eighteenth century. The pigment, formed from the reaction between the two chemicals, was used in paint and laundry bluing and has a blue green hue.

French blue or **ultramarine** was originally obtained from the semi-precious stone lapis lazuli and has a warm, violet hue. Lapis lazuli has been used since ancient times for mosaics and other inlaid work, carved ornaments, vases, and many decorative objects. An artificial substance that is much cheaper to produce has now largely replaced it.

Cobalt blue, a compound of cobalt oxide, aluminium oxide, and phosphoric acid, is like ultramarine but a less intense color. **Cerulean blue** is another compound, this one made of tin and cobalt. It is an expensive pigment to produce and has a turquoise green tone.

Moods of blue

Blue is one of the colors linked with calm and tranquillity, and is associated with the elements of the sky and water. It is thought by many to be a spiritual color, often linked with meditation. It is believed that being surrounded by blue can help lower blood pressure and relieve insomnia, which makes it ideal for a bedroom.

Blue is also thought to aid recovery, promote healing, and relieve pain, and has been linked to good communication and clear thinking. It may, however, cause some people to feel cold and, if at the dark end of the spectrum and not lifted by brighter colors, could lead to feelings of depression and loneliness.

Green is perhaps the most versatile of all the dark colors; it works well with both contrasting and compatible tones as well as many others from the color wheel. It can be used to create environments with diverse appeal, from simple country rustic to jewel-like, gilded opulence.

Greens tend to fall into two categories: those with vegetable origins and those that reflect the colors of more precious objects and gems. Apple, cabbage, fern, lime, ivy, olive, and pea all have their roots firmly in the ground and belong in the first category; agate, malachite, celadon, and jade belong to the second. The names given to the shades complement the various images and styles that the colors can be used to conjure, from the more everyday forest and bottle to the luxurious emerald and jade.

You can create the tone-on-tone effect in a room by taking a deep green, such as forest, as the main color and accessorizing with paler shades, such as celadon and mint. But avoid overdoing the greens as you may make the room appear monotonous or like a claustrophobic box. Also, green gives a message of organic stability rather than a brilliant or exciting message, so it is vital to inject other colors and shades of black and white to give depth and variety to the scheme.

ESTABLISHING A CONTRAST

To find colors that contrast with green, look at the other side of the color wheel on page 33—you will see the color red. This may at first sound like a traffic light combination, but if the colors are used together in the right quantities you will find that they are opposites that attract. If you mix red and

Shades of green vary from the everyday cabbage, pea, and apple to the more luxurious tones named after precious stones, such as emerald and jade. Within each there is a variety of depths to inspire a scheme. For example, the pale yellow green of an inner cabbage versus the dark outer leaves, as shown on the left, and the varying greens of malachite stone, shown at right.

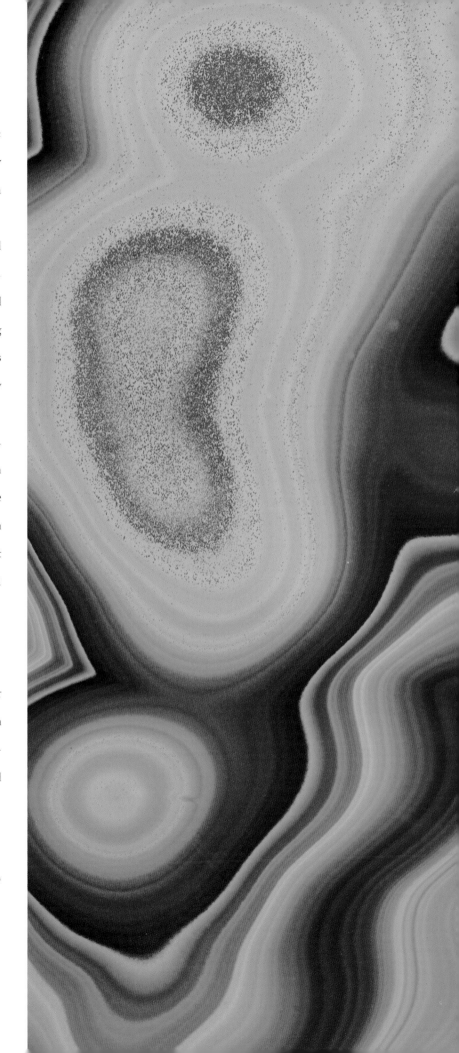

green pigments you get a brownish tone, so you may find that even bright red tends to look a little duller when put beside green.

Think also of nature, with its green leaves and red flowers and berries, and the more tropical and exotic watermelon and papaya, with green skins and red or pinkish flesh. Nature's color schemes can be a useful guideline, but be careful and choosy about the depth and brightness of colors. Make sure there is plenty of dark green and also paler shades of green to counteract the hotness of red or other vivid colors you may choose.

If your green has a predominantly yellow base then so should the red, which should lean toward the orange rather than the blue side of the spectrum. If the green is dark, then the red should be of a similar, more muted, tone or the contrast will be too extreme. You can also use corridors or narrow bands of shades such as white or black to create thin but important breaks between the two colors. Black can be used like a mock shadow, giving depth and outline to the colors, whereas white will lend a feeling of space and light.

Accessories such as cushions and throws may be used to give seasonal changes to a green scheme. In the winter, you may choose to play up the depth and richness of green by incorporating covers with deep silk, velvet, gold twisted fringes and braids, and red-and-green tartan cushions or striped throws. In summer, the look can be made cooler and fresher with white-and-green checked covers and touches of lemon, orange, and other citrus colors in throws, cushions, and vases of fresh flowers. A theme could also be taken

RIGHT: *In this room, a pale shade of green has been used above the dado rail and a deeper, richer shade beneath. This is a useful way of introducing a dark color to a scheme without making the overall appearance of the room too heavy; it is also a clever way to make a tall wall appear smaller.*

from a floral motif, which will provide pattern and a variety of color against an existing, plain green background. For example, if the floral has soft, pastel colors, these can be highlighted by adding plain cushions and throws to complement the colors within the design.

LOOKING BACK IN TIME

To see how effective the combination of dark green and its contrasting color, red, can be, and to get an historical perspective on this combination, it is worth taking time to study some of the works of the great artists. In Anthony Van Dyck's painting *The Balbi Children* (*c.* 1627), for example, a large forest green banner hangs down between two classic columns and the subjects of the portrait, the children, are dressed in black and bright red. They stand out against the background, yet are in harmony with it. The banner acts as an unobtrusive point of focus, leading your eye to the subjects and acting as an intermediate level between the back and foregrounds.

Green has long been a color favored for decorating and there are many historic examples. At the fairytale castle of Chenonçeau, in France's Loire valley, the walls of Catherine de Medici's study are covered in a leaf green jacquard fabric. With windows overlooking the countryside beyond the castle, the effect is to give the room a strong sense of being in harmony with the landscape.

OVERLEAF LEFT: *The reflective sheen on the surface of this black upholstery fabric gives it a luxurious appearance and also helps to reflect light, giving definition to the curves and shapes of the padded areas. The black provides a strong contrast against the muted green of the wall.*

OVERLEAF RIGHT: *The reflective surface of this painted floor doubles the effect of the daylight from the adjacent window. If the floor was covered in a dark, matte, pile carpet it would absorb the light and make the room appear darker.*

ABOVE: *This cozy sitting room feels intimate and secure; the pale-colored furniture prevents it from feeling too oppressive. The oatmeal shade of the upholstery is repeated in the check of the curtain and in the background of the painting over the fireplace.*

LEFT: *Pale-colored furniture and soft furnishings are more noticeable against deeply colored backgrounds. Here, the contrast of dark and light colors also emphasizes the unusual shape of the ceiling and links the lower section to the tongue-and-groove paneling above, making the dark wall appear taller.*

Green was often found in Victorian rooms, such as the library of the famous English collector Sir John Soane, which has a mix of green and red. Likewise, William Morris's bird-and-fruit design *Strawberry Thief* features a strong green element with blue and red. The fabric and wallpaper featuring this design are still popular to this day.

USING PAISLEY AND TARTAN DESIGNS

Other schemes using green and red can be based on Paisley and tartan fabrics. Paisley designs incorporate the teardrop motif, which is seen in shawls and fabric from countries as diverse as India and Scotland. The Paisley design was used in wool shawls made in the town of the same name in Scotland, but the motif is found just as often embroidered in gold on saris in India, or in fine cashmere and wool shawls from Kashmir. It is also found in some of the brightly colored fabrics of the Provence region in the south of France.

The Scottish Paisley designs often use rich, warm colors: red, plum, and raspberry, with dark greens and blues. The Indian fabrics tend to be in cream and lighter shades, but against a plain green upholstered sofa, a throw or cushion cover in this design will become a feature.

Generally speaking, tartans dominated by the color red are from Highland clans, but the red is also said to be linked to many of the families who followed the Catholic faith. Among the best known are the Stuart, McBean, and McClean tartans.

Other tartans that have only a very fine line of red or no red at all will often feature deep green and blue. For example, the Johnston, Black Watch, and Gordon tartans all have deep green, blue, white, and yellow, although predominantly the darker colors. The hunting tartans of most clans, including those whose dress tartans feature red, are usually dark and strongly green. This was used for camouflage when out hunting stags in the forest or the clan's enemies in the heather, rock, and bracken-covered countryside.

You may also come across pale tartans with light blue, pale sage green, and pinkish reds. These colors are often derived from tartans that were buried when the English king forbade the wearing of the plaid after the battle of Culloden in 1746. The cloths, dyed with vegetable and mineral dyes, were buried or hidden away; when they were unearthed, following the lifting of the ban in 1782, the colors had faded.

In a dark or rich green room, a tartan carpet can give a strong Scottish overtone without being overpowering; tartan fabrics are also available in upholstery- and curtain-weight materials, so they can be used on soft furnishings. Otherwise, woolen rugs in a variety of similarly colored tartans can be used to create a Highland feel.

COMPATIBLE TONES

On either side of green are the compatible shades of yellow green and midblue. Blue and yellow combine to form green, and are thus green's "parent colors." Contemporary textile designer Tricia Guild has used this combination of closely related colors with great effect in many of the distinctive fabrics produced under the Designers Guild label. Many shades of these colors have a fresh, bright, modern feel.

The fashion and interior designer Anoushka Hempel has a black and green room in her home. The walls, which are painted a rich malachite green,

The classic wood paneling in this hallway has been painted a yellow-based green, which is fresh and linked to colors found outdoors, beyond the front door. The decorative carving of the dark wood chair becomes a feature in its own right and practical elements, such as boots, scarves, and walking sticks, sit comfortably against this backdrop.

ABOVE: *Large French windows and a small circular window allow ample daylight into this room, while directional or task lighting, such as the flexible shell shade light on the piano, adds a rich and focused golden glow. The decorative cameo paintings on the wall lighten the expanse of blackness.*

LEFT: *The type of surface finish you choose when using deep colors is important. The sheen on the surfaces of this darkly painted hallway reflect light so that it feels less enclosed and heavy. The white balustrades on the staircase also lift the scheme, and the mirror reflects and enhances available light.*

at first appear to be mottled or dappled. But on closer examination you can see leaves and branches of an abstract forest. Against this background she has set black and gold furniture and accessories, chosen to create an opulent and dramatic effect.

To make a scheme that is opposite to this opulent richness, use green with white, a combination that is fresh and clean. In fact, the white adds a zest that a dark green on its own may lack. Green-and-white gingham check can be used in a rustic scheme with pale or midtone wooden furniture, basketwork, and flag or terra-cotta tiles on the floor.

Similarly, green-and-white stripes can be used in a Nordic or even Regency-style scheme. For the Nordic interpretation, wooden furniture could be limewashed to take the edge off the brown and then overpainted with fine lines and decorations in deep green to add a touch of embellishment. The floor could be covered with limewashed pine boards and painted around the edge to create a frame or border.

For a Regency style, walls could be painted in dark green below the dado and white above, with lines of gilding used to accentuate the level of the baseboard, dado, and picture rail. An elegant chandelier and glass wall sconces would add light but luxurious details, and regimental green-and-white striped fabric would be ideal for curtains and upholstery.

The advantage of deep greens such as holly and emerald is that they look good not only with their contrasting and regular complementary colors but also with many others because green is a "natural," almost neutral, color. For example, purples such as lilac and violet can be used to great effect with a strong, dark green background, as can certain tones of yellow, although a tone that is too vivid will bring out the acidity in the green.

TONE ON TONE

If using a tone-on-tone basis for your decorative theme, splashes of unexpected colors will add interest and a change of pace. Using small quantities of the colors in cushions, throws, borders, or curtains can create a more contemporary edge and a less predictable finish to a room.

When choosing colors that do not comply with the basic rules of color matching, take good size swatches of the base and other colors and see how they appear together in daylight—both morning and afternoon—and artificial light. In this way, you get a good idea of whether or not they are compatible before you commit to the scheme.

As well as having contrasting accessories, you may also like to consider having two tones of green on the walls. For example, you might cover a windowed wall, and perhaps an opposite wall with a fireplace, in a color a couple shades lighter than that used for the remaining two walls. The paler color on the fireplace wall will reflect the light from the window, creating a frame around the fireplace and making it the focal point of the room. The same effect will be created on the window wall, although curtains will

OVERLEAF LEFT: *This hand-painted, climbing, leaflike design is in keeping with the nature-inspired shade of green used on the walls, and is in contrast to the large black-and-gold geometric panel that stands in front of it. The panel appears more solid and dominant against the soft, feathery background.*

OVERLEAF RIGHT: *The dark wall enhances the paler, golden objects set in front of it and enriches the colors of the portrait that hangs upon it. Directional lighting, such as a picture light, will further augment this effect.*

RIGHT: *A white cornice divides the dark green walls and ceiling and creates a visual break in this expanse of dark color. A picture rail, parallel with the top of the bookcase, provides another division. Bright orange upholstery, a gilded decorative light, and a mirror frame also lift the overall appearance of the room.*

have to be draped around corbels or contained by tiebacks so that the maximum amount of wall can be seen. By using the paler color on the walls that are dissected and interrupted by features, the two remaining dark walls will make the overall scheme appear predominantly deep and rich.

Mixing paler tones with darker ones can also be used to accentuate the height and features of a room. For example, the area below the dado could be in a rich dark shade, the dado itself picked out in white, the area above in a midshade of green, with a white picture rail above and the ceiling in white or a hint of green. This scheme will make the room appear taller and lighter. Painting the ceiling dark green and doing the scheme in reverse will make the ceiling seem closer and the room smaller.

WHAT'S IN A SHADE?

There are shades of green that are associated with specific places and locations. For example, Lincoln green and Kendal green are both believed to have been named after the colors local cloth was dyed in these rural areas of England. Lincoln green is perhaps best known as being the color of the clothing worn by the legendary Robin Hood and his Merry Men, the green being a helpful disguise in their forest lair.

Camouflage greens are found in military combat gear. The browns and greens are printed in irregular patches to create a pattern that is hard to distinguish from undergrowth or woodland. Camouflage colors such as khaki go through fashionable phases, but tend to be too muted and earthy to be the main or dominant color in an interior scheme.

Rich dark green is a color often associated with gentlemen's clubs and sports rooms, the green being the color of card and billiard tables. The color is said to be restful and calming but also acts as a good background to the brightly colored billiard balls and white-faced playing cards with black and red markings. Lights suspended above these tables often have green glass or brass shades to restrict the flow of light. This leaves the rest of the room dimly lit, with light focused on the table surfaces and games in progress.

SETTING THE TONE

An oriental Zen-style theme can be created using soft greens, such as bamboo, teamed with a rich green like dark jade. This can be accessorized with simple bamboo furniture and celadon-green glazed stoneware. Celadon pottery from China was once a royal favorite for vases and incense burners and is a classic ware; the pottery is a greenish gray that has, in fact, given its name to that particular shade

For a classic, grand, and opulent style that endorses the richness and gemlike qualities of emerald green, accessories must play a vital role. The room itself can be simply decorated, with the four walls and even the ceiling painted in a high-gloss green finish, although a gilded picture rail or cornice will be needed to give some definition to the upper reaches of the room. Against this background, pieces of glittering glass, gilt, and silver will stand out and, when illuminated by candles or low-voltage spotlights, will sparkle like gems. Black and gilt period furniture will look gracious in this setting, as will curtains in satin-finished jacquards or with gold wire thread.

A light, natural floor covering, pale furniture, and well-chosen window treatments—here, a rolled-up blind and curtains draped around the outer frame of the window with tie-backs—ensure that the rich wall color does not make the room feel small or dark, but instead adds a touch of luxury and impact.

Against dark green walls or under upholstered furniture in the same rich tones, flooring will provide an important background. If the walls are a rich dark green, avoid flooring in the same color as it will make the room feel as though it lacks a base or grounding element. By all means choose a carpet that has an element of green, but not one that is a single, plain expanse.

As green is the color of nature, it can be effectively teamed up with natural materials such as stone, marble, and wood, for the floors. A yellowish Bath or York stone will complement the yellow element in the green, and coir or sisal floor coverings are equally suitable.

Green wood stains can also be used to give faded or stained plank flooring and furniture a new lease on life. Because of its earthy origins, green works well as a dye color on wood. Many of the wood stains available can be diluted, so you can vary the depth of shade for an effect that is subtle. This will allow the wood grain to show through, which can be effective in a wood-themed kitchen or study.

In old houses there may be a room or hallway with paneling, in which case a rich green stain will provide a colorful yet sympathetic covering. If there is no paneling you could create a *trompe l'oeil* effect by painting or staining lighter and darker lines on a plain background to emulate the curves and sections of beading used in real panels.

LET THERE BE LIGHT

Lighting in this type of opulent room setting is very important. First, dark colors tend to absorb rather than reflect light, so the positioning and power of the artificial light has to be carefully calculated. Dark shades may look dramatic in an opulent scheme but they will also reduce the effectiveness of a lightbulb.

If you do have dark lampshades, make sure they have a reflective inner surface. For example, a black shade with a gold lining will give a rich yellow pool of light on the surface directly beneath. A golden or ochre-colored glass shade will appear richly yellow when not illuminated, and when the bulb beneath is switched on it will glow and allow light to pass through the glass as well as underneath.

To make the most of the available natural light, use mirrors to reflect the daylight and double its effectiveness. By keeping curtains and blinds well away from the frame of the window you will also increase the amount of natural light coming into the room. Remember, too, to keep climbing plants and foliage trimmed away from the outer edges of the exterior of the window as this can also restrict light flow.

As with the blue rooms, the quality and quantity of lighting in a room with a predominately dark green scheme is influenced by the surface finishes. Felt, a popular green fabric, will absorb light, as will velvet. But the shiny surfaced satins and some silks and chintz finishes will reflect a certain amount of light, so a mixture of fabric finishes will be useful, as will midlevel table lamps that will highlight areas around armchair and sofa height where most cushions and upholstery fabrics will be arranged.

Leather, with its slightly shiny surface, looks good in a rich green finish and will make excellent long-lasting covers for sofas and dining room chairs, especially in styles such as the classic, buttoned Chesterfield. Leather tends to improve with age; as it wears and mellows it becomes more attractive.

A stripped, light wood floor and pristine white painted bookcase and mantlepiece contrast with the deep bottle green of these sitting room walls. Old books and paintings sit comfortably against this color, as do flowers, which have an affinity to this earth-related shade.

ABOVE: *Shades of green and its parent colors, blue and yellow, can be used together to great effect. Each of these cabinet drawers has been painted in an individual, rather than a matching, color, which can help when it comes to identifying the contents. It also makes the drawers a feature of the room rather than just a utilitarian piece of furniture.*

RIGHT: *The rough wash of green paint on this broad, paneled wall has a worn, antique appearance that is compatible with the style of furnishings and artifacts displayed against it. This type of textural painting can be used equally well on floors and furniture.*

THE SOURCES OF GREEN

Leaves, grasses, roots, and lichens provided much of the early green dyes, but now the variety of shades available through chemical colorants is enormous, and they have a clarity and consistency never available with the rather muted natural dyes.

*The green dye properties of **grass** and **lichen** can easily be seen on the white clothes of ballplayers who have dived across the field to catch a ball, or on small children who roll down grassy banks and climb trees on a summer's day. To extract color from leaves, grasses, and lichens, armfuls of the basic ingredient had to be gathered and then boiled or ground. Boiling would break down the outer layer of the plant and eventually, after many hours and much evaporation, provide a powdery substance that could be stored and used at a later date. Other pigments were extracted by grinding, the lichen or grass being placed in a pestle (a small stone bowl) and pounded by a mortar (a small, hand-sized stone).*

***Earth green**, a natural pigment containing manganese, is a soft mossy green that doesn't give much depth of color. This natural coloring is rarely used for paint or textile dying, and the synthetically produced shade is better as a background color for walls or carpets than as a color with which to highlight an architectural feature or accessory. It is a restful, calm shade but lacks intensity.*

***Chromium green** is also a pale green, but has more intensity than earth green and can be used as a background color against which gilded frames and dark wood furniture will look good. This shade has earthy overtones but contrasts well with black and brown. The more vivid greens, such as **emerald** and **forest,** can be made with a base of phthalocyanine. This pigment is a comparatively recent discovery, being introduced in 1938.*

Moods of green

Many of the rich and deep tones of greens invoke ideas of woodland or forests and can have olfactory links with fresh cedar and pine aromas. The forest and nature connotations can also encourage feelings of calmness, tranquillity, and growth.

Depending on the shade and depth of green, various moods can be created. The more vivid, bright greens seen in fresh new leaves and crisp apples are colors that invigorate and lift the spirit. They can bring a feeling of cleanliness and promote a more optimistic outlook. Also, being in the center of the color wheel and the rainbow, green is said to have a balancing effect and can restore equilibrium.

The smoky green of celadon was a popular choice for porcelain and pottery glazes in Thailand and China. It was believed that the celadon glaze had the ability to change color if it came in contact with poison, so it was used in the homes of high-ranking families and officials to ensure that their foods were safe to eat.

Jade comes in various shades, from a deep mossy green to a pale minty hue, and has a soft, almost muted, buttery quality. Jade is one of the oldest and most curious of all precious stones, and the color is associated with wealth and fortune. In India it is also regarded as sacred, and in the past green jade could only be worn by the royal family. In China, a newborn baby has a jade bracelet placed on its arm, which should be worn throughout its life to bring good luck.

The calming effect of green is also used in the "green room" of a theater or television studio. Originally, the green room in the theater was painted that color to give the actors' eyes relief from the glare of the stage lights; nowadays it is a room where guests and interviewers meet before going on stage or on air.

Green is also a color linked to many superstitions and beliefs. It is used to represent gladness, immortality, and the resurrection. In heraldic devices, green is referred to as vert and denotes love, joy, and abundance. Among the Greeks and Moors it was the color of victory, and in some churches and religions it is used to represent God's bounty. It is also the color used to represent the planet Venus and in metals it indicates copper, which turns verdigris (or pale green) when it weathers and ages.

Green is a color with many qualities. It can be used in backgrounds or accessories to bring a calm but lively atmosphere to any room, and can feature in schemes from opulent to rustic.

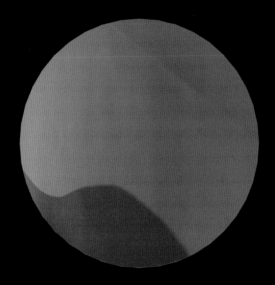

REDS & PURPLES

Red is the color of passion and fire, of warning and rage, yet it can be a relaxing and enjoyable color to live with, whether used in just a single element, such as a bowl of deep red roses, or at full volume, with walls and ceilings in a rosy hue.

Red is the color of passion, blood, lover's roses, and berry-flavored wines. It is also the color of danger, revolution, and anger. It is a dramatic color and not one for the weak spirited.

Red is a color that should be handled with care when decorating. The brightest shades, such as vermilion and scarlet, can appear to exude warmth and can cause the occupants of a room to feel overheated and irritable. Some may find it makes them feel anxious and hemmed in. But when used with other colors that dilute its heating effect, red can be an elegant, dramatic and rewarding color in the home.

Red varies from deep, reddish brown terra-cottas to rich berry reds; it can also be vivid, like scarlet, or more subtle, like raspberry. On the color wheel its contrasting color is green, as mentioned in the previous chapter, and its companion colors are yellow reds—such as orange or gold—and blue reds, such as crimson.

Red is one color that you have to be careful with when designing a tone-on-tone scheme. The lighter and darker shades of the main color should always contain the same base note. For example, if you are taking a blue red as the main dark color, lighter shades should also contain the blue tone. If you pick lighter shades from the yellow red side of the compatible range, then they will not sit well; they will inject a yellow note against the blue, which in this case may be too complex.

If you do want to mix yellow red and blue red elements, make a link or create a rainbow effect so that there is a graduation of tone in the color.

ABOVE: *Red and green are often found together in Scottish tartans and more modern checks. They are diametrically opposite each other on the color wheel, but when used in balanced quantities can be a fresh and lively combination.*

RIGHT: *Although thought to be colors that clash, pink, red, and orange can be dramatic when used together. The key is to keep a similar hue or base tone in all the shades you choose and to mix elements of each together, as shown here in the cushion covers and curtain trim.*

OVERLEAF LEFT: *The petals of a rose demonstrate that in nature there are many variations in the tone of a color. These dark and light contrasts can be used to create areas of light and shade within a scheme.*

OVERLEAF RIGHT: *The texture and composition of a material will affect the way it is seen in different lights. For example, the smooth, shiny finish of silk will reflect light whereas the matte surface of a dark-colored felt will absorb it. This in turn will make the surfaces that the fabric covers appear glossy or dull.*

For example, a row of cushions could start with bright pink (which has a blue element), then go to a soft lavender pink, a plain blue, a green blue or turquoise, a plain yellow, and finally an orange red. This rainbow provides a ground note for each side of the color spectrum. A multicolored throw containing this mix of colors can also be used to bring all the elements together.

A deliberate clash of colors can also be fun and interesting. For example, against the neutral background of a white wall, vivid yellow red upholstered furniture can be lifted with cushions and throws of bright orange, vivid green, and yellow. The red will provide a constant background color and the bright individual colors will act like sparks of color against it.

TEAMING AND TONING

When thinking of tones of blue red and colors that complement them, take inspiration from nature and the dining table, from overripe raspberries, burgundy and claret wines, and the plump lusciousness of juice-laden plums. Think of the things that complement these fruits and drinks—for example, raspberries served with cream, especially a rich, yellow, clotted cream. Claret

PREVIOUS PAGE: *This exotic bedroom makes use of the tone-on-tone effect of using differing strengths of the same color and immediately related colors. This type of scheme is harmonious and can be created using a mix of plain and patterned fabrics.*

RIGHT: *This red wall appears as a panel framed by white surrounds; the white confines the color and reduces its intensity and volume. Although most of the furnishings and artifacts are in neutral colors, a red cushion is used to link the interior of the room to the dominant wall color.*

FAR RIGHT: *Black, red, and gold is a combination that has regal overtones. Here, floor, walls, curtains, and part of the upholstery are all in red, but the gold dots on the walls and curtains prevent the scheme from appearing monotonous, and the chair's back trim adds depth and defines its shape.*

and burgundy wines are drunk with cheese, which again has creamy, yellowish tones, and once you bite into the deep red skin of a plum, a succulent golden-yellow fruit is revealed.

For a grand, opulent look, red is usually teamed with gold—gold being the orange and yellow red side of the companion colors' spectrum. Silver on its own can look too white and pale against the heat of red, but may act as a cooling element if mixed among gold accessories. Crystal, chandeliers, and richly patterned fabrics will all add to the grandeur.

In the chic and majestically decorated Café Marly at the Louvre in Paris, the walls have been painted with a matte pillar-box red over a black background. The upper layer of color has then been rubbed in places until the darker shade shows through. This creates an aged effect that also reduces the redness and adds depth and interest over a large wall area, which might otherwise be monotonous. The doors and woodwork are painted black and details, such as the paneling on the doors, is picked out in a burnished gold, heightening the feeling of richness.

You can also cool red down by adding earthy tones, such as grays and browns. Gray walls with white woodwork and red furniture can be minimalist in style but still make a statement. Rich mahogany and cherry wood furniture or polished floorboards will complement the red of brightly painted walls but also provide a much-needed calming element.

LEFT: *Red can be a womblike, relaxing color, and with subdued, golden lighting in a bedroom it is restful and warm. Black is a dramatic partner for red, but also has a cooling, calming influence in schemes dominated by the fiery shade. Here, the billowing curtains add to the feeling of luxury and richness.*

ABOVE RIGHT: *Red upholstery and curtains contrast with darker colored walls to make this room appear vibrant and interesting. The same color has been picked up in the background of the coverings on the sofa and cushions, tying the accessories in with the main piece of furniture.*

OVERLEAF LEFT: *A red note is present in most of the colors used in this room, although some shades have a strong blue bias. The effect is modern yet rich, and combined with the suede paneling on the walls and deeply textured upholstery fabrics, endorses a sense of opulence.*

OVERLEAF RIGHT: *This simple yet interesting contemporary scheme uses the same red on the walls as on the upholstery, which gives a feeling of unity, as though the seat is part of the wall. The graceful curving shape of the sofa is also highlighted because the covering is plain; if it was patterned the eye would be drawn to the fabric rather than the shape of the furniture.*

ABOVE: *In this artist's living room, an opulent terra-cotta red provides a backdrop for various works of art, some framed, others left unmounted. The wall color appears to reduce the scale of the large, airy room, making it feel more comfortable.*

RIGHT: *Red is a color that has long been associated with picture galleries, as many paintings respond well to being hung on a background of this color. Gilt frames stand out well against red and seem to accentuate whatever feature they surround, whether a work of art or a mirror.*

THE FULL POWER OF RED

There are certain places where the full intensity and vibrancy of red is needed. Robust hues are useful in cold hallways of old country houses, or in dark rooms that don't get much direct sunlight. Rooms that are used only at night or for formal evening entertaining are also good places in which to use red.

Red has been popular as a decorative color in dining rooms for many years. There is even an historically-based paint color known as Eating Room Red, which was popular in the mid-nineteenth century and was made possible by the discovery of new pigments. This shade looks best at night with candle- or subdued electric light, which makes it come alive. By daylight it is still attractive, but lacks the depth and drama that artificial illumination creates.

Dark red walls or furniture in a formal reception area or in entertaining rooms is said to create a warm, intimate atmosphere that is relaxing and reassuring for guests. In an office or business reception area, red walls may be a bit overpowering but a red mat, a vase of red flowers, or a couple of red scatter cushions could make it feel less formal and more welcoming.

As red is a color often linked with royalty and grandeur, the use of red wall coverings and upholstery can be an easy and comparatively cheap way of making a simple space feel affluent, even if it isn't. The color conveys these concepts subliminally, and because it gives off an aura of warmth it can also imply a richness of surface and finish as well.

Picture Gallery Red is another color that has been popular for centuries, long used for the walls of grand halls and libraries. The main galleries at the Royal Academy of Arts in London have red walls, providing a perfect backdrop for paintings framed in black and gold. Portraits, landscapes, sculpture—especially those of white or gray marble—all work well against a softly muted red background.

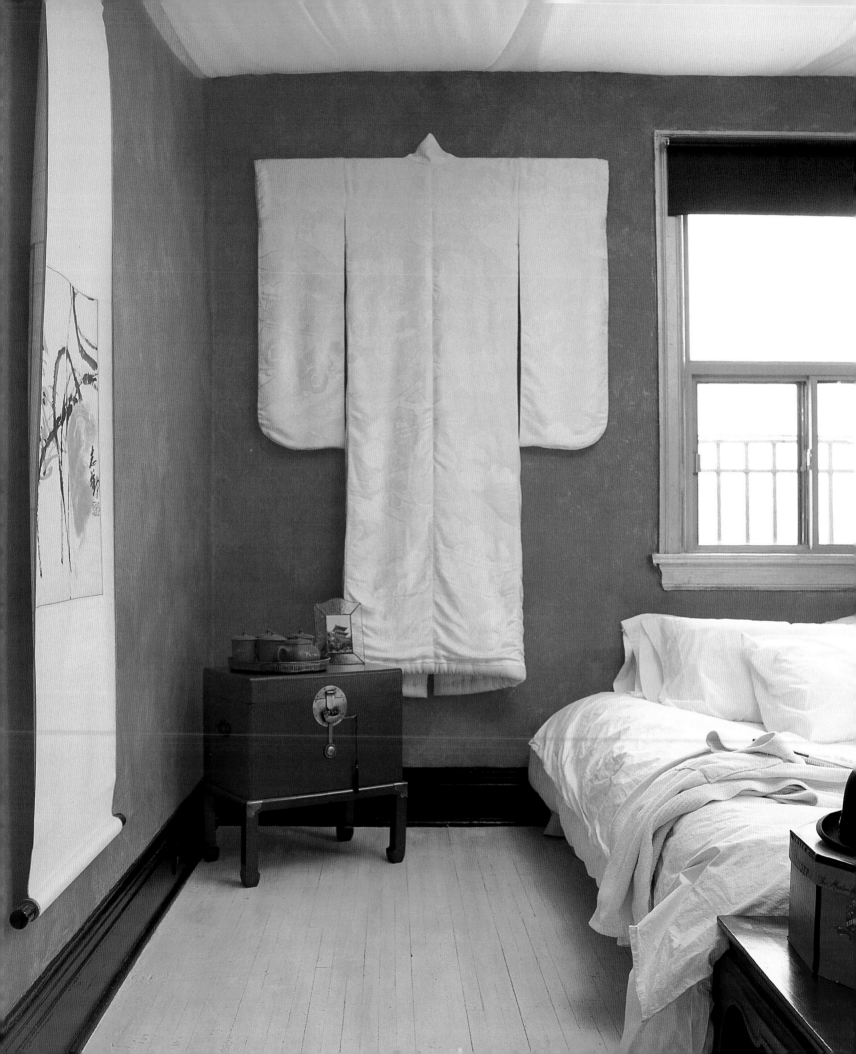

Landscape artist Julian Barrow, who is based in a turn-of-the-century building of artists' studios in London's Chelsea, has red walls in the studio where he lives. He believes that it is a perfect color to use as a background for almost any style of painting. It also makes his lofty, north-facing studio with large windows feel warmer and more intimate.

Flat, featureless walls painted in a single shade of red can be easily decorated with beading to create a paneled effect. Simply paint the walls in silk finish and the strips of beading in a gloss paint so there is a contrast in surface appearance rather than color. Pictures can be hung to line up within the faux or real panel, so that the beading of the panel becomes a secondary frame, giving extra emphasis to the picture.

THE ETHNIC STYLE

Red teamed with black can be used to create an oriental feel, especially if the finishes are lacquered or have a glossy shine. This combination can be very effective in a minimalist scheme with just a few well-chosen objects on display, such as simple pieces of black furniture, low-level boxes, and tables. The scheme is reminiscent of the lacquerware produced in China as it reflects the same hot-cold, opposites-attract balance found with yin and yang.

LEFT: *Red is a color that has oriental associations; it is often seen in lacquerware and partnered with black in decorative objects from the East. These red walls are finished with a black gloss baseboard, and at the window there is a simple black blind. The furnishings and decorations are minimal but the room still looks complete.*

RIGHT: *Terra-cotta red is a color that occurs frequently in ethnic pottery and ceramics because in many areas it is the natural color of the local clay. The clay may also be used to render walls, so the pigment also becomes the room color. The plain walls here stand in contrast to the decorative floor tile and cupboard.*

ABOVE: *The yellow wall is in harmony with the red but also acts as a counterfoil to the intensity of the color. The two areas are visually linked by the linear metal wall sconce and the linear metal chair, as well as the pale wood flooring that runs between both.*

RIGHT: *Well-placed lighting is vital in dark-colored rooms. These small, recessed spotlights cast beams upward onto the red panel, creating areas of light and shade. Downlighters and a table lamp illuminate the fabric blind in the window and the white wall beside it, providing a contrast to the red.*

Another ethnic-inspired scheme could be built up around carpets. Red is a dominant color in many kilims and rugs from Turkey, North Africa, and northern India, and a red carpet is a good way of adding a warming element to a cold flag or stone floor. Not only will the softness and texture of the carpet add an element of comfort underfoot, but the color will also help.

Kilims or kilim-print fabric can be used to upholster chairs, sofas, and footstools, and to make various cushions. To take the Moorish, Turkish or eclectic ethnic mix further, add polished brass bowls and tables—the brass being a compatible goldlike element—and hang rugs on the walls. The walls could be painted in a deep red matte to complement the colors of the hangings, and lighting could be provided by wall sconces of cut-out metal that cast interesting patterns and shadows around the walls and ceiling.

A TOUCH OF RUSTIC

At the opposite end of the scale, red can also be used to evoke a rustic feel. Red-and-white check or gingham is used for tablecloths in wayside bistro restaurants in France and in pizzerias and pasta restaurants in Italy. In France, the look is complemented by small pictorial lace curtains that hang in the lower halves of the windows, and in Italy by a Chianti bottle made into a candle holder; both will have either a terra-cotta tiled floor or plain wooden boards.

A more general country style can be created with red-and-white gingham curtains and cushion covers, white walls, and furniture painted in a bright red. Elements of green, such as green-and-white china on a dresser and plants on the windowsill, will keep the overall scheme fresh and light. This is especially important if the scheme is used in a kitchen, where a large stove may make the real ambient temperature high and where the addition of too much red in the decorative scheme could be overpowering.

THE POSITIVE

Natural floorings such as sisal and coir have a yellow-gold element that looks good with both the yellow reds and blue reds. Animal skin-style rugs also suit this rich color, and with the many excellent fake fur and printed hide replicas that can now be found in shops, there is no need to endanger any wild species. The dramatic black and white of zebra stripes and the golden brown of leopard markings can bring an exotic element to a red room.

The expression "getting the red carpet treatment" means that you are treated as a VIP, someone special. You can give yourself the red carpet treatment every day by fitting one in your own home. The thing to be wary of, though, is that a plain carpet is more likely to show stains than a patterned one, and if your carpet is in one of the brighter yellow red shades, it will mark more easily than the deep black and blue reds. Any plain single-colored carpet should be protected with a stain-repellent finish that has a branded and recognized guarantee.

A plain red carpet next to a plain red wall might be too much of a good thing, especially in a larger room where there are expanses of both surfaces. The scheme is more likely to be effective if you break up one surface with a pattern or stripe. For example, the walls could be papered or painted in a red-and-black stripe and the carpet in a plain red, or the walls could be in plain red and the carpet in a red-based tartan.

If you are adamant that you want walls and floor in a plain version of the color, a black or similarly contrasting color on the baseboard will create a break between the two surfaces. You could also add black dado and picture rails to divide the walls' area into smaller, less dominant sections.

INTRODUCING TEXTURE

Pattern can be introduced in many ways, but fabrics are generally the easiest surfaces. Curtains, blinds, cushion covers, and throws can all be decorated with woven or printed designs. As with green, there are many tartans that offer useful geometric, red-based designs. Paisley prints can also be used, many of which favor the blue red colors rather than the vivid red.

Self-patterned damask and jacquards have an opulent feel and are suitable for the more classic schemes. They are useful for adding a little texture and pattern without introducing another color or prominent design. Red velvet has the most opulent feeling; it is the color of cushions that support royal crowns and glass slippers in fairy tales.

Velvets come in many varieties, from the luxurious and expensive silk velvet to the less pricey synthetic varieties. Velvet can also be plain or patterned, with designs printed or embossed onto the surface of the pile or created by leaving areas of the fabric without any pile, the latter known as *dévoré*. For a lavish setting, cushions in each of these types of velvet could be arranged on a daybed or sofa.

Red furniture is generally painted or lacquered. Earthy brown and blue reds are found on the painted chairs and cupboards of the American Shakers as well as many utilitarian pieces found in Scandinavian homes. The dining room in the home of Swedish artist Carl Larsson has furniture painted in deep red and green as well as a lighter, more orange red. This gives the impression of warmth when the snow is piled up outside.

Despite all the warnings about living with red, it is a color that gives great pleasure and there are many people who, having lived with a red room

---

Color is not confined to walls. Here, a red highly lacquered floor provides a warm base to a white room. Objects and furniture placed on this floor look strong and clean. The vibrant red also resonates, giving off a reflection that warms the cool whiteness of the walls.

ABOVE: *Softer shades of red, such as raspberry and damson, have a tranquil and comforting quality. These colors have a cooling blue element in their composition, which makes them useful in bedrooms. They also mix well with silver and other blue-toned silver metals.*

LEFT: *Some tartans have a predominantly red background but also incorporate other colors, such as yellow, blue, green, black, and white. If you want to use a variety of colors with red, a tartan fabric may give you a good palette. By using the tartan for curtains, upholstery, or a carpet, you can link all the elements together.*

in their home, would never be without one. Red has survived all fashions and trends and is a color that can be used in both traditional and contemporary settings, although the balance and choice of the color's tone may vary.

INTRODUCING LIGHT

Lighting rooms that are predominantly red is usually less difficult than the darker blues and greens because it is a color that does not absorb so much light. This is particularly true for the brighter and more yellow colors; when you veer toward the blue reds, they start to take on the absorbent qualities of blue.

Yellow reds are the best shades for rooms that are used mainly in the daytime. The yellow in the red will make it bright and lively; it will also respond well to natural light. The bluer end of the red spectrum can look dull in natural light, and may require additional artificial lighting to lift it, even during daylight hours.

The blue reds respond best to artificial lights and nighttime locations. Light can be used to highlight features in a room, making them stand out against the darker colored walls. It's not so easy to achieve this effect with the yellow reds because the tone is lighter, although you might get the effect by directing spotlights onto gilded frames, brass, and other shiny objects.

Tinted lightbulbs are available in good design and electrical shops, and some have a warm pink tint that can be used to add extra richness to a pre-dominately red scheme. However, don't be tempted by red lightbulbs as they emit little light. They are really for Christmas decorations and party purposes and will do nothing to embellish a domestic setting.

Various shades of red can be used together in a decorative scheme, but it is best to keep to the same family of colors—either based on a yellow or a blue note—so that there is harmony among the shades. Yellow reds tend to be fiery and hot, so are best reserved for use in accessories or in public and daytime rooms.

THE SOURCES OF RED

In Ancient Egypt, Persia, China, and India, red dye was obtained from various earth and plant sources as well as animal blood. As time passed, other shades were added to the palette. These more complex pigments were derived from insects, shellfish, and minerals. Among the most successful and best known of these natural sources are the shells of the insect cochineal and the root of the herb madder.

*The pink red of **cochineal** was made from the crushed dried bodies of female insects reared on cacti in Mexico. This was an expensive color to produce, and was highly prized for fabrics used in clothing and decoration. **Madder** is from the herbaceous plant Rubia tinctorum, which has yellow flowers, and was a more widely available colorant. This dye is extracted more easily, directly from the plant's root.*

***Vermilion** was used in Europe from the eighteenth century. The color is very bright, with a slight orange tint, but the original pigments were unreliable and over time the brilliant red tended to darken toward black.*

*After 1856, more chemical-based colors were made and tones such as mauve, magenta, and crimson appeared. **Alizarin crimson**, first produced in 1868, replaced madder as a strong, reliable pigment useful for glazed finishes. **Cadmium red**, composed of three parts cadmium sulphide and two parts cadmium selenide, was first created in the 1920s and has a hot orange undertone.*

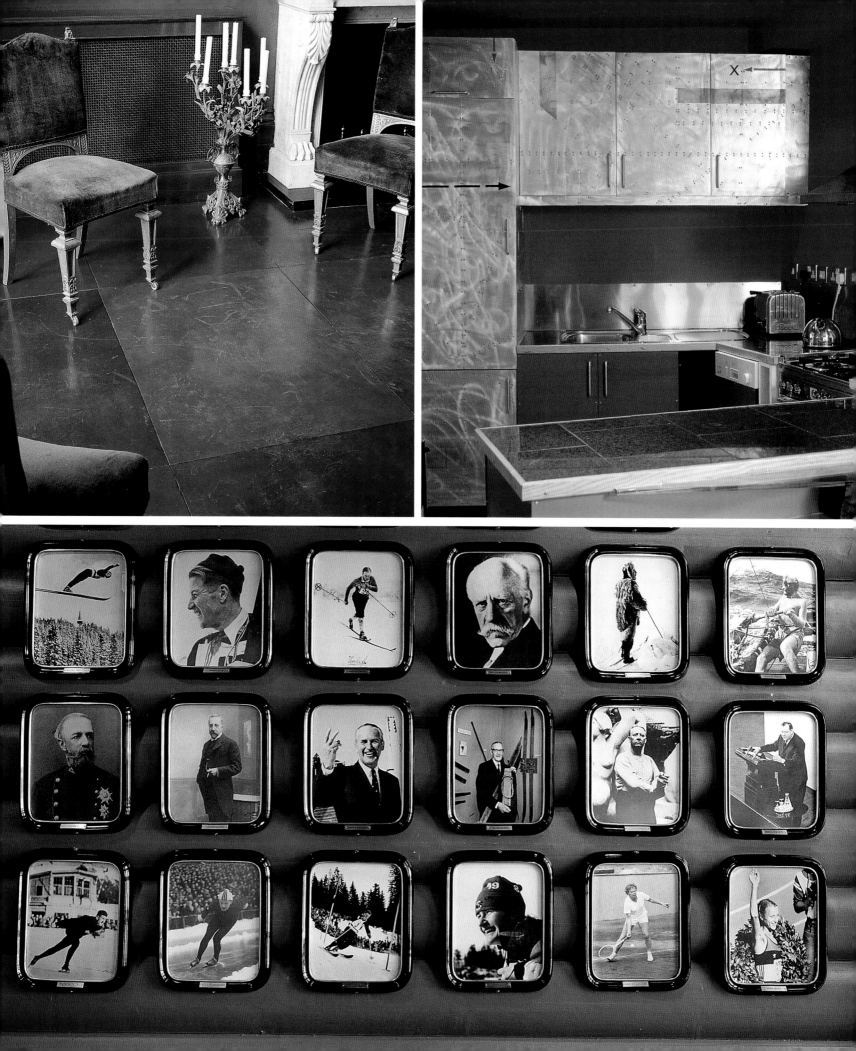

Moods of red

Red is a color that should be handled with care. The brilliant shades, such as vermilion and scarlet, have connotations of being red hot, angry, or dangerous and may, when used in quantity in a room, cause the occupants to feel overheated, irritable, and even bad tempered. But mixed with black or blue the color becomes calmer and more opulent, and can create a womblike feeling of security and peace.

Red is a color that is said to help poor circulation. Sitting in a red room or wrapped in a vibrant red blanket will psychologically make you feel warmer and more secure. It is also reported to revitalize someone who feels lethargic, and to improve energy levels.

It is said that by painting your front door red or placing a red mat or runner in a hallway you will make guests and visitors feel welcome. In feng shui, a runner or large mat can act as a symbolic bridge or link from the door to the private, inner sanctum of the home.

Red flowers or a red candle are also said to be auspicious, although there are some who firmly believe that red and white flowers should never be mixed because they are said to represent blood and bandages. As such they are particularly inappropriate to bring as gifts for someone in the hospital or who is recovering from an illness.

Red is one of the three primary colors (along with yellow and blue), and can thus stand alone in its pure state without having to be mixed or blended with other pigments. In heraldry, red is referred to as sanguine and denotes magnanimity and fortitude. In church decoration, it symbolizes martyrdom. In metals, it represents iron, the metal of war; in precious stones, the ruby represents red; and in planetary realms, it represents Mars, the god of war. In folklore, red is the color of magic. It is also the color of radicalism, socialism, and revolution.

Purple is made by mixing together quantities of red and blue. The resultant tones can vary, from shades of aubergine and amethyst to blueberry and blackberry. Purple tends to be a color that provokes a strong reaction and arouses pleasure or aversion: You either like it or you don't.

The color opposite to purple on the color spectrum is pure yellow, a primary color. Compatible colors on either side are crimson and violet blue, and although not strictly within the main family of compatible colors, green is also a good partner. As mentioned in the chapter on green, it is a color of nature and in many ways a neutral; if chosen in tones compatible with purple, green can be used to create an unusual but elegant scheme.

Because purple is a dominant and intense color, you may find it easier to use in panels, on a single wall, or in a secondary role, such as on upholstered furniture or soft furnishings. To create a paneled effect, you could paint within the border of beading in a strong shade and then use a lighter color, such as lilac or a rich cream, for the rest of the wall area.

The paler cousins of purple, such as lavender and lilac, tend to be linked with trendy phases, such as the Flower Power era of the 1960s, but true rich purple is perennially popular among lovers of deep colors. Purple has the warmth of red but is less overpowering because of the addition of blue in its makeup. It is a color that invokes a feeling of luxury but can be tempered or moderated by adding paler-colored elements that dilute the mood.

Purple also has bohemian connotations; it is often seen as being a socially unconventional color found in the homes of writers, artists, and people with a free-and-easy attitude to life. Bohemian crystal from Czechoslovakia can also be found in shades of purple.

The pinks and purples used on this wall, tabletop, and candles are an example of tone-on-tone arrangement. The colors have a common base—in this case, red and blue—but are mixed in different quantities so that some lean toward the blue side of the color wheel and others more toward the red.

HISTORICAL CONNOTATIONS

Purple is linked with the 1920s—the Roaring Twenties—and the decade's fashionably attired Flapper girls and theatrical cliques. It was a color of drama and opulence in this post-World War I era, when the pendulum swung away from austerity toward the lavish and luxuriant.

Purple was also popular with Victorians. The first synthetic mauve dye was created in 1856 by William Henry Perkin, and with this invention mauve became cheaper and more widely available. It was also popular for a time because it was the color of mourning, and with the death of Prince Albert at the age of 42 in 1861, his wife Queen Victoria went into deep mourning and remained in virtual mourning for much of the rest of her life. Although the country did not embrace her grief to the same extent, the color became more widely seen and hence used.

An interesting purple brown, ripe-fig color was popular in Georgian times and can be seen on some of the old buildings in London's East End. The color was used both indoors and out and was mixed from a combination of pigments. An old wooden dresser and built-in shelves painted in this color can look particularly effective when set against accessories in the silver gray of pewter and the pinkish red of old Cranberry glassware.

In Roman times, purple was a color of status and importance as it was decreed by Gaius Julius Caesar that the color was to be worn only by the Imperial family, members of the senate, and the nobility. The color was so expensive and precious that most togas were only edged with a band of the color to acknowledge the status of the wearer.

COLOR COMBINATIONS

Purple isn't just a historical or faddishly trendy color; it can also be given a strong contemporary edge by mixing it with vivid yellow (its contrasting color), lime green, and orange accessories. These zesty colors have a common

yellow theme running through them and will stand out against the richness of a purple background.

To highlight the royal connections, purple can also be teamed with bright red. This works well if you put a couple of red cushions on a sofa or armchair upholstered in purple. The effect is dramatic, strong, and unexpected.

For an opulent, decadent look, cool silver—rather than warm, yellow gold—can be used to great effect with purple. This combination of silver or chrome with purple will convey a balance of heavy and light, rich and cool, which will suit a paired-down but extravagant setting. It will be a chic, minimal style rather than a basic, aesthetic version.

For example, a room could be decorated with two deep purple walls and the opposing walls in white. In front of the white walls, a sofa is covered with a loosely fitting blue red linen cover, and in front of the purple wall another sofa is upholstered in the same way, this time in a silvery, white gray linen. The rest of the furniture could be in chrome, glass, and black, with a bowl of rich purple anemones on the mantlepiece or a white-and-black border surrounding the fireplace.

The Scottish architect and designer Charles Rennie Mackintosh created a version of this color combination and style of design in the early 1900s. His furniture, often in an exaggeratedly tall, linear style, was usually painted white or black and was occasionally decorated with delicately colored stencils of stylized flower patterns and simple insets of purple amethyst glass. Although his work is often classified as Art Nouveau, it avoided the excess found in some continental designs. His premise was that he rejected the over-decorated Victorian style in favor of a spare simplicity that featured geometric shapes and unadorned surfaces.

For a more conventional dressed-up and sumptuous look, you could have two walls in a purple with a strong red emphasis and two with a bluer note, though balanced in tone. Dress the walls with ornate gold

ABOVE: *The intensity of purple will vary according to the light source. Check your choice of color in both natural and artificial light in order to gauge the difference before committing it to your walls.*

LEFT: *The walls of this bathroom have been divided in two, the lower section in a red-based orange color and the upper in a deeper, more plummy shade. At night this room becomes the perfect place for a relaxing bath.*

wall sconces, a central golden chandelier, and curtains with a purple pattern embossed on a pale gold background. The chairs could be French Empire style with ornately carved backs. If the room is a dining room, the table could be set with fine white china plates edged with a regal purple band with a gold outline—a setting fit for Napoleon himself.

Purple is said to have a meditative quality, and the bluer shades a relaxing and therapeutic effect. Therefore it can be a good color to use in a bedroom or private relaxation space. The addition of purple can also be a useful way of warming up shades of blue. For example, a bathroom decorated with a mix of purple, lavender, and dark and pale blue tiles, and with the rest of the walls painted in a lavender blue, will appear warmer than with the pale and dark blue on their own. These colors all have a common base color, and by introducing the warming red element of purple you counteract the coolness of the blue. Purple is a color rarely seen in a kitchen, and seldom in tableware, except as a small decoration or border.

Gray is another color that works well with purple. Like silver and pewter it offers a harmonious and attractive accompaniment. This combination is especially effective in the nongloss finishes, such as silk and matte paints, which give the colors a powdery, almost textural, appearance.

It's all in the finish

If you are really passionate about purple, then paint your walls with a high-gloss purple finish. The hard, shiny finish may make the purple seem darker and deeper so be sure to try a sample area to check that you get the shade of color you really want when the gloss has dried.

To dilute a strong shade of purple, place white with it. Paint effects, for example, can be used to retain the strength of the original color while softening its overall appearance. Deep purple paint can be dragged with a dry scrunched-up cloth or wide, hard-bristled paintbrush over a white painted background so that the deep color is spread thinly, leaving areas of white revealed. This enables the background color to reduce the power of the topcoat without actually making it a paler color.

If you find that white is too much of a contrast, try using an off-white or cream, both of which are just a little warmer than white. If you are using a predominately red purple, ensure that the cream has a warmish red tint, too.

Colorwashing is another good way of easing a strong color across a surface. The secret to achieving this effect is to keep the sponge or brush fairly dry and to work the color out from the point of application with repeated strokes. Gently draw the color away from the central point so that it becomes more and more diluted; this should be done smoothly so that there are no visible lines or joins. The finished effect should be cloudlike and look aged and slightly weather-beaten. There will be patches where the full-strength color is seen, but others where the color is much paler and less intense.

Choosing soft furnishings

For curtains and upholstery, fabrics such as deep-pile velvets will intensify purple's feeling of warmth. Silk is a yarn that is particularly suited to purple as the smoothness of the finished cloths, such as silk satin, seems to suit the opulence of the color. In Roman times, both silk cloth and the color purple were kept exclusively for use of the royal and aristocratic families.

Purple is a color that comes in and out of vogue, and is one that you either love or hate. Here it is used to highlight a gently curving wall, bordered by a simple but strong black floor and a neutral, white wall. As purple can be a difficult color to work with it is often best used as a single panel or for accessories.

In contrast, light, simple white voiles and fine cottons can be used in more understated schemes. For example, white blinds or softly draped curtains can be trimmed with a border of purple satin ribbon or broad cotton braid to give them a smart and regal look, or just to help tie them in with the rest of the room. White or cream muslin could also be over-printed with a random, simple motif, such as a *fleur-de-lys* or polka dots, to take an element of the color through from the walls to the window dressings.

Heavy, deep purple curtains are not a good idea unless you have a room with many large windows because the fabric will absorb light and, when pulled back, their furls and folds will cut down the access of light through the window. If you do want to carry the color through to the curtains, look for a patterned fabric that mixes the dark purple with others so that it is a linking, but not overpowering, element. For a regal setting it could be mixed with a gold or silver thread, or a golden thread in a sateen stripe. For a simpler effect, dark purple could be diluted with a paler shade of the same color, such as lilac or white, which will add a fresh, clean touch.

Furniture covered in rich royal purple upholstery looks good against golden wood paneling. Purple leather seats are also complementary to pale, honey-gold wooden chairs, as well as to more angular black designs. Painting furniture purple is a dramatic step and may suit a scheme in which purple is used as a secondary element. Using purple chairs and tables against purple walls will be overpowering and may make the furniture seem to disappear.

LEFT: *In this bedroom, a plainly painted wall has been given regal appeal by the addition of gold, stenciled* fleur-de-lys. *The sheer opulence is echoed in the shiny satin bed throw.*

RIGHT: *Purple with more red than blue becomes this warm damson color. The embossed pattern on the velvet cushions reflects the wall color against the deep blue pile of the background. The purple theme is carried on through the bed throw, where it is mixed with a rainbow assortment of other colors.*

LIGHTING IT UP

A purple scheme with a red emphasis can be cooled by adding pale blue trimmings or accessories, while a cool, blue purple can by warmed with the addition of red-based accessories. The paler shades of raspberry, lilac, lavender, and cherry will all help to redress the warm/cold color balance and introduce elements of lightness to a dark background.

Lighting the bluer shades of purple will have to be carefully managed as the blue will have a tendency to absorb the light and the room will need to be well and adequately lit. The more red there is in the color, the hotter it will be and therefore the less absorbent, although with purple a blue element will always be present.

The type of lightbulb used in a purple interior is very important. Lightbulbs with strong yellow elements may make deep shades of purple appear black, while bulbs with blue tints may make them seem too cool by enhancing the blue element of the color. Daylight bulbs are often the answer to this problem as they will emit a light that will keep the color as close to the original as possible.

If you have used a rich purple on the walls, then it is best to opt for a light-colored floor covering; a dark one may make the room feel boxlike and the walls appear closer together. If you have an existing dark wood floor then the baseboard and woodwork in the room should be picked out in a lighter shade. This need not necessarily be white but a warm off-white, cream, or pale purple shade that picks up an element of the color of the wood and is complementary to both it and the walls.

LEFT: *Some plum and deeper shades of purple can have an almost brown appearance, which works well with creams and other buttermilk and coffee colors. Dark amethyst purple is a color that looks particularly good on velvet, satin, and other sensual and opulent fabrics.*

ABOVE: *With its regal associations, purple is often found in state and court robes, edged with ornate embroidered braids and trimmings. The edge of a curtain, cushion, or chair cover can be given a throne-room-like appearance with appliquéd or stitched gold or sliver detail, fringing, or cord binding.*

THE SOURCES OF PURPLE

*In the early days of the Roman Empire, garments colored with **Tyrian purple**, a dye derived from a shellfish of the Mediterranean Sea, were worn by the Imperial family and the nobility. This purple dye is said to have been discovered by the Phoenicians, and was exported from a city and seaport in southwest Lebanon, now known as Sidon.*

*In the fifteenth century, a purple dye was developed from a local lichen in northern Italy, and during that time the area became the dying center of Europe. And in America, especially the eastern states, the **poleweed** or **pokeberry** (Phytolacca americana), which grows to 10 feet (3 m) tall, has purple berries that contain a powerful purple dye.*

*But it was Englishman William Henry Perkin who oxidized **aniline** and obtained the earliest synthetic dye, known as aniline purple, or mauve. With his father and brother he set up a factory producing mauve dyestuffs and was knighted in 1906.*

*Among the chemical dyes now used to produce purple is **manganese sulphate**, a pink crystalline solid prepared by the action of sulphuric acid and used for coloring cotton, and **potassium**, which is used for both textiles and leather.*

Moods of purple

The mood created by a purple-dominated environment will depend entirely on whether the color is more heavily biased toward blue or red. More blue will make it a cooler, calmer color whereas more red will increase its hot and fiery aspects. Purple is said to be a color that brings passion into rooms where it is used.

Purple is also recorded as being a stimulant to the brain, and is believed to promote creative energy. It is thought to have spiritual qualities, which can help in self-discovery, and can be a good color for a room where contemplation or meditation takes place.

While Napoleon I was in exile, the violet was adopted as his emblem. "Père de Violette" became his nickname and small bunches of the flower were hung up in the houses of Frenchmen who supported their hero's cause. The flower and the color are still associated with the Bonaparte family to this day.

Purple is the color of royalty and justice, and in heraldry it denotes temperance. Among metals it represents quicksilver, and in precious stones it is the color of amethyst. The planet Mercury is also represented by the color purple.

BROWNS

Because this color is often associated with wood, it is always present in our homes, but there are passing trends for darker and lighter shades, from the passion for stripped pine in the 1960s and 1970s to the interest in Wenga and the almost-black, tropical dark woods in the 1990s.

Brown, like green, is a color of nature; it can be earthy and base or glamorous and rich. Tones vary from the tasty-sounding chocolate and toast to the earthy burnt umber. There are a variety of shades available that reflect the color of woods and forests—mahogany, teak, cherry, cedar, and redwood—as well as those, especially among the paler shades, that are simply mouthwatering, from toffee to mocha. These paler tones, along with mouse, mink, and mushroom, can be used to bring a softer, less woody, accent to a dark brown scheme.

Brown is a tertiary color; it requires three elements—red, yellow, and black—to be mixed together to obtain the one color. The primary colors—red, blue, and yellow—appear as they are, and the secondary colors, such as violet, orange, and green, are made by mixing two colors together. But many of the colors that are created by mixing three or more elements tend to have looser names allotted to them by paint companies, each using its own variation on the theme or what is currently in vogue.

Brown can also be obtained directly from a pigment such as sienna, a color that was originally made from the reddish earth around the Italian town of that name. Umber and burnt umber were also made from a natural clay, which was roasted to achieve a deeper, blacker brown.

The use of brown as a main color in a decorative theme has, as with the paler shades of purple, been subject to fashionable whimsy. It was another popular color of the 1960s, frequently seen teamed with orange in swirling psychedelic prints or as a carpet matched with magnolia-colored walls in homes across the country. But, also like purple, brown has come back into vogue. Not only have the 1960s-style geometric prints now made a come-back but, when used in various shades, brown has become the trademark for classic, understated chic.

Internationally renowned Italian designer Georgio Armani has used shades of brown to create wardrobes of tasteful fashion. The subtle combination of brown and cream has became his trademark, and many people now refer to these as "Armani colors."

Taking the lead from the catwalk, many interior designers and fabric companies have produced compatible shades of browns, which can be used together to create different levels and depths in a scheme. For example, dark browns, such as chocolate, can be lightened with a tone-on-tone palette of taupe, beige, cream, caramel, and coffee, or can be made warmer by adding redder and darker tones of spice browns, such as cinnamon, nutmeg, and clove.

In a scheme such as the tone-on-tone brown one described above, the quality of the materials used and the standard of decoration should be high. There are no bright elements or opposing colors to distract the eye, so the line of vision will be taken to the finish and minutiae of the room. The soft restfulness of such a room is created by its lack of stimulus or vivid contrasts, which means that focus is concentrated on the detail.

ACHIEVING A VARIED TONE

In these single-color decorative themes, where the variation is introduced by tones of the parent color, texture becomes an important way to avoid monotony. Mix rough with smooth and patterned with plain, as well as adding interesting accessories such as polished coconut shell bowls, sparkling

In addition to the wood colors, brown comes in a variety of food-inspired shades, from milk and plain chocolate to cocoa and coffee. These inspirational colors can be teamed with bright orange or pale blue for a modern look, or with cream and white for a more classic style.

RIGHT: *A pale wood contemporary console table sits on a light ash floor, balancing the incipient darkness of the cocoa-colored walls. The leaflike upholstery fabric on the chair combines pale cream with a darker outline, echoing the dark and light elements of the walls and floors.*

FAR RIGHT: *Chocolate-colored walls are teamed with white for a colonial-inspired theme. The woven cane bedstead keeps a light feel to the furnishings and crisp white bed linens brighten the overall appearance. Cream leather suitcases and accessories provide a color bridge between the contrasting white and brown.*

OVERLEAF LEFT: *Dark colors can be used to great effect as a background to highlight architectural features within the home. This ornate, gold-painted metal balustrade makes an otherwise simple staircase a focal point, with the brown wall emphasizing its curving shapes and reflective finish.*

OVERLEAF RIGHT: *Dark, chocolate brown Wenga wood is used as panels to conceal closet space in this bedroom. The doors have become an integral part of the decorative theme, their color picked out in the trim of the pillowcases on the bed.*

ABOVE: *This mottled, mouse brown wall has a muted, almost suedelike appearance, making it a neutral background that would work in tandem with most colors. The soft gray blue of the door frame, which has a similar depth of color, provides an unexpected but favorable contrast.*

RIGHT: *The dark colors and low light in this room give it a tranquil and calm ambience. The long, dark brown curtains could look drab, but against the rust color of the walls they are rich and compatible. The wall and curtain colors can also be seen together in the framed bird prints.*

glass vases, elements of gilt or silvery gold, and tortoiseshell effect or amber to accentuate the earthy provenance of the main color. In this way a room will be calm and harmonious, but interesting.

Because of brown's neutral and natural coloring, the texture of brown fabric takes on additional importance. From rich dark browns to cappuccino colors, tactile quality is an integral part of the finished scheme. Rough linen and hairy jute as well as warm cashmere, smooth silk, and deep brown wool all contribute to an interesting array of texture.

Brown is a neutral shade with which most other colors are compatible. It can be used with colors that may be difficult to match, such as turquoise and shocking pink. It is also a versatile color, one that can be easily warmed or cooled by the addition of red or blue. A proportion of green or yellow can also be introduced so that the brown will have an affinity with the accompanying color used in a scheme.

This versatility makes brown an interesting color to work with because there are few rules governing its use. There are a number of unlikely combinations that have to be seen together to be appreciated. For example, as mentioned in the chapter on purple, a brown with a purple hue can be a very interesting and unusual color; it can be teamed up with purple or violet accessories and those with a pinkish red to raspberry bias.

Another unusual but effective pairing is brown with blue. Pale duck-egg blue can be especially attractive and restful, while a vivid electric or peacock shade will make a startling and interesting contrast. This latter combination has a fresh and contemporary feel and can be used in a low-key, minimally furnished room because the mix of colors is attractive and different.

The warmer side of the color wheel can also be effective with brown. Red, orange, and yellow will complement its red and yellow base notes and the brightness of these colors will create a cheerful setting. A rich cream with a yellow base note is also a good companion color for brown. As with

OPPOSITE: *The walls of this room have been divided so that the lower paneled area is in light-reflective and contrasting white, while the area above is in a deep chocolate brown. Dark furniture and accessories have been included to bring an element of the deep brown to the lower, brighter area.*

LEFT: *A wall of dark brown velvet curtains discreetly conceals a spacious closet area in this bedroom. The texture, folds, and softness of the fabric prevent the volume of dark color from becoming too dominant and solid.*

purple, think of food combinations—chocolate cake with cream, brownies made with creamy white nuts, ice cream with chocolate sauce—and cream, unlike white, is not such a harsh contrast.

By adding red tones to a standard brown, the color becomes hotter and more vibrant. These chestnut tones are warm but not as overpowering as undiluted red. They can be used in schemes with a spicy element and exotic decor, complemented by room scents of cinnamon and star annis—in a seductive bedroom, for example, with rich satin and velvet cushions and throws in dark, rich browns and reds.

Red browns also come into the terra-cotta category, the color that is most associated with rustic and Mediterranean designs but can also be found farther south in the medinas and markets of Morocco and North Africa. Terra-cotta mixes well with the fresh colors of white, green, turquoise, blue, and opulent gilt tiles, and could be used to create a room with a Marrakesh theme. The red element in the composition of terra-cotta can be enhanced so that the rich aspect of the color is emphasized. Terra-cotta will also work well with polished brass accessories, lightweight voiles dyed in cool tones of mint green, and daybeds scattered with cushions.

OVERLEAF LEFT: *Orange and red are colors that are compatible with brown; orange, which contains elements of red and yellow, takes on a brown appearance as it becomes darker. Here the dark floor provides a base for the brighter, hotter colors above.*

OVERLEAF RIGHT: *The white baseboard and door frame define the floor and door area in this chocolate brown scheme. The reflective surfaces of the mirrored table and cocktail shakers look crisper against the dark surroundings.*

LEFT: *This dramatic hallway has high-gloss, dark brown walls that are illuminated by spearlike wall lights and small overhead spots. The mirror at the end of the hallway returns the light and gives an impression of greater length, which prevents the space from becoming boxlike. Pale floor coverings and a light curtain also help to make the corridor feel lighter and more roomy.*

BROWN FINISHES

There are a number of decorative themes that have been inspired by brown, the most obvious of which is wood. Tongue-and-groove wooden planks can be used to create the feeling of an Alpine-style chalet or a North American wood cabin. Dark wood-paneled walls give a sense of solidness and grandeur and are a perfect foil for mirrors and pictures in gilded frames. Pictures that are in black and white should be surrounded in bright or light mats to help them to stand out against the background.

Dark wood beams or paneling, like those found in a cabin or converted barn, combined with brown and white or brown and cream can be a charming color mix, but another color should be included to keep the scheme from becoming too flat and dull. A patchwork quilt in a bedroom or a *toile de jouey* print will be light and fresh and will bring the colors together.

Brown fabric wall covering can also be effective. A self-patterned jacquard will keep the emphasis on the color but offer variation in pattern and surface finish, having areas of matte and others that are more shiny.

Modern suedelike material is also attractive in brown. A deep shade will have the illusion of being like cocoa powder, and will have an inviting tactile quality. Rather than cover four walls with faux suede, use it on a single wall or panel for dramatic impact.

Wood paneling has been mentioned, but leather is another old-style finish that has come back in fashion. It would be expensive to cover walls with leather, but a single panel on each wall could look effective. Leather floors are also becoming more popular.

ABOVE: *There are many faux paint finishes and effects that can be used with a brown scheme, such as tortoiseshell, marble, wood grain, and metals like distressed bronze and faded gilding. New, shiny brass light stands or wall brackets can be given an aged appearance with brown glazes and waxes.*

Another fabric that must be mentioned here is silk, especially shot silk. Shot silk is made from a warp thread (running top to bottom) in one color and a weft thread (running left to right) in another. Brown woven with a vibrant orange or rich red will make an opulent combination. The shot fabric will change color depending on which way you look at it. In one direction, the brown will be dominant; in the other, the orange or red will shine out. This material will also respond in a magical way to good lighting, and is especially effective in the evening when illuminated by artificial sources such as candles and chandeliers.

CREATING AN ETHNIC-STYLE INTERIOR

Being derived from the earth, brown is a popular ingredient in ethnic designs. Rich, red brown and yellow ochre shades are frequently seen in native mud cloths and mixed with black in other designs. By using a scheme based on the warmer shades of brown and mixing a generous quantity of yellow you can create a room with overtones of the heat and sunlight of a far-off country.

To accessorize this native look, there are many interesting dark wood-carved masks and wooden spears that can be hung on reddish or ochre brown walls. Amber, the yellow brown fossil resin that has a sweet scent when rubbed, also has a compatible earthy element, and although amber itself is expensive, amberlike glass is quite easily sourced. Tortoiseshell is another substance that has an affinity with this sort of scheme. Although the real tortoises and turtles from which the shells were originally taken are now protected, there are many imitations and copies that create the same effect.

For those who prefer a concentrated blend of the warmer, more spicy shades of brown, a spice merchant theme could be a good route. This is a perfect way of bringing together an eclectic mix of foreign artifacts and colors—with elements from India, Malaysia, and the Far East—and setting them against a mid- or reddish brown background.

Brown is also a popular color for ethnic pottery because local clay is used to create the vessels. In France, brown bowls are often glazed with a yellow or cream finish, and in the south around Provence a rich olive green is common. In Italy and Portugal, the more decorative wear is painted with white and sometimes blue; everyday tableware it is left in its natural color but is usually glazed to make it waterproof. Mexico and other parts of South America also produce simple clay pots as well as masks and plaques.

Using the earthy browns of these rustic potteries could be an interesting way of developing a scheme. For example, if you take the brown and green pottery of Provence, consider what might follow. The *tournesol* (literally "turn to the sun") sunflower is a popular flower grown for its seeds and oil. The sunflower is yellow with a dark brown center; yellow, green, and brown are all yellow-based colors, so they create a harmonious mix. The textile prints from southern France feature these colors together, and so the decorative idea can be continued.

WAYS WITH BROWN

For walls there are number of interesting alternatives to standard paint and patterned papers. Good-quality lining paper can be stained with tea or coffee to achieve a faded, parchment look that will give a room a feeling of history. Diluted tea or instant coffee can be sponged or brushed onto the paper on the wall and left to dry. Start with a light first coat and then, when it is dry, apply another coat, building up to the intensity you desire.

Mirrors can be a useful way of bringing extra light into a dark-colored room. This mirror reflects the illumination provided by the pendant light in front, as well as that of the candle opposite and the wall sconce at the side.

Simple, utilitarian brown paper can also be used as a wall covering. This old-fashioned wrapping paper can be bought in industrial-size rolls direct from the manufacturers or through a good stationery supplier. The quality of the paper should be good, with a slight sheen and a faint stripe. It is best to buy a large roll that will cover all your wall area because there may be slight variations in coloring between batches. The paper will also appear darker and redder when wet with paste, but when it dries out the slight sheen and fine stripe on the surface will reappear and the color will become paler.

If wood paneling exists in a house it is a wonderful asset, but it is expensive to install from scratch. However, you can achieve the effect with scumble paint and some beading. Section off the wall into regular-size areas and apply narrow bands of beading to create the panels. A traditional style is to have a tall panel above the dado rail and a smaller square one below.

Once these have been put in place the whole wall can be painted to look wood-grained. This is best done by a specialist decorator, unless you are very talented and artistic. The paint effect is created by painting an oily glaze over a base coat. The glaze is then combed with a metal or wooden comb to create the ridges and lines seen in the grain of wood. A feather may also be used to emulate the oval eyes or knots found in panels and planks. This technique was very popular in Victorian times and can still be seen on doors, door and window frames, and pieces of furniture from that time. On furniture, a faux bamboo pattern can also be found.

Another faux effect that is often found using shades of brown and burnt sienna is marbling. The entrance lobbies to many old hotels and municipal buildings are decorated with what looks like fine Carrara marble but is in fact the handiwork of a local decorative painter. Marbling, like faux graining, is a job that requires skill for the paint effect to look good enough to trick the eye of the beholder. It is best to follow the instructions in a specialist paint effect book and practice on paper or old pieces of scrap wood before starting on the real thing.

The main area where most amateurs fall down when painting these effects is in the blending and mixing of colors. It takes many tones of brown, white, and even flecks of yellow and red to create an authentic-looking marble. The other downfall is that people tend to add the darker, uneven lines like flashes of lightning across the wall and do not soften or merge the dark colors with the surrounding paler ones.

MOVING ON TO THE FLOOR

Wooden floors are an asset in any home as they can provide a cheap and easy way to alter the floor covering. First ensure that the wood is in good condition and that it is not infested with woodworm or any other pest. If there are damaged boards they should be replaced, if possible, with reclaimed boards of a similar size and appearance. If the floor has been covered, you may also need to strip away any adhesive or backing that remains from tiles or linoleum, and if carpet has been laid over the floorboards there may be nail heads that have to be removed or hammered farther into the wood.

Once your wooden floor is prepared there are a number of ways to treat it. If the wood is old, of good quality, and mellow, it may simply require a good cleaning and an application of polish or varnish. If the color is too pale or dull, a good quality tinted varnish or wood stain will revive it.

On a rich brown wood floor you could also add a border detail. This can be a simple band of color applied in paint or a deep color stain. A border

Brown walls don't have to be painted. This expanse of wood-paneled cupboards creates a solid color feature, with the grain also introducing an element of pattern and contrast. Although the floor is in wood of a similar tone, the recessed base provides a definitive break between the two.

around the edge of the floor can be decorative and imitate marquetry or inlay; it may also be an elaborate stylized pattern or repeated motif.

If the floor is of a cheap or unattractive wood you could stain it to look like mahogany or an expensive hardwood, or simply paint over it. It could be painted in a single plain color or in a simple geometric pattern. To create a checkerboard pattern, you can either work with a stencil or use masking tape. Divide the floor into squares and paint in one color. Allow it to dry, adjust the tape to border the remaining squares, then apply the second color. When all is dry, seal with a durable varnish. This can be a useful way of creating definition between wood-paneled or brown walls and a brown floor.

To lighten a dark brown wood floor, you can sand off the existing finish and apply a soft limewash of emulsion paint. This allows the grain to still show through, giving the overall effect of an old, now pale-colored floor.

Natural floor coverings such as coir, jute, and sisal have an earthy element in common with brown colors. The light golden coloring of the matting also has an affinity with wooden furniture and paneling, and suits both contemporary and traditional settings. Kilims and oriental rugs look superb against natural wood floors.

LIGHTEN UP

Lighting brown walls and surfaces depends a lot on the depth of color and finish. If you opt for a fabric wall covering, such as mock suede, then the light needs to be strong and plentiful because both the color and the finish will absorb light. If, however, you opt for a high-gloss finish or a red brown, then there will be a certain amount of reflection that will help to increase the effectiveness of the light.

A brown room can look darker in daylight, so choose your color carefully and avoid shades that have a black or deep blue note, which will emphasize the dulling effect. Browns with a creamy or yellow base will be warm in daylight, and if used with a cream or yellow ceiling and a light floor covering, such as cream tiles or coir matting, will not be oppressive.

The neutral and natural coloring of brown makes the texture of brown fabrics take on added importance. From rich dark browns to the pale caramel and cappuccino colors, the fabrics' feel and tactile qualities are integral parts of the finished scheme. Rough linen and sisal as well as warm cashmere, smooth silk, and deep brown wool, will all contribute to an interesting array of texture.

Brown furniture is widely available, simply because so much is made from wood. There are traditional pieces such as four-poster beds, chests, benches, and tables, which have been around since medieval times. These old pieces tend to be dark and aged. The more important ones often have a date or pictorial element engraved into one or a number of the surfaces.

Lighter and more modern wood furniture tends to be golden or pale. Biedermeier furniture in the late neoclassical style combines light woods with black ebony or stained wood detailing. Utilitarian pieces made from the cheaper soft woods can be stained and polished to give them the appearance of more expensive, classic pieces or painted so that the brown color is obliterated.

Although a whole dark brown room may be a little overpowering, rich brown shades are useful as backgrounds or supportive colors. Dark brown is one of the colors that can be used as a single feature or to highlight, rather than dominate, a room.

There are many interesting and unusual types of wood. Most of the rarer varieties are now grown in managed plantations to prevent overcropping of natural forests. The grains, textures, and color variations in wood can be inspirational when planning a brown-based scheme.

SOURCES OF BROWN

Browns with red hues include **sienna,** *named after the source of the best quality clay containing iron and manganese, found near Sienna in Italy. There is also* **raw sienna,** *which is a lighter tan brown, and* **burnt sienna,** *a richer deeper, ox-blood brown.*

Raw umber comes from clay with a higher manganese content than sienna, giving it a cooler, greenish overtone. **Burnt umber** *is made by roasting the raw umber to produce a deep black-red color.*

Ochre is another brown that comes from an earth source, being found in natural clay colored by iron. Its shade varies from a brown yellow to a red brown, depending on which part of the world it comes from.

MOODS OF BROWN

With its earthy roots, shades of brown are restful, reassuring, and grounding, although too much brown can be oppressive and depressing. The lighter shades of brown, such as mouse and mink, tend to have a softness that is gentle and heartening, and which can help relieve anxiety and restore confidence.

GRAYS & BLACK

*Grays and black may initially be thought of as dark and depressing shades,
but when used with white and vivid colors they can be dramatic, and a
perfect foil for more outrageous schemes.*

Gray is not a color but a shade, like black and white. Undemanding and tranquil, it is easy to live with. Grays vary from deep dark tones, such as charcoal, to light silvery shades that are just off white. Gray is useful as a background because other colors and black and white stand out against it and, as with brown, small amounts of other colors can be added to a basic gray paint to make it more harmonious with a companion color.

For example, a basic black-and-white mix can be warmed with a touch of red or made cooler with the addition of a little blue. Yellow will give it a slightly more green appearance and brown will make it earthier.

Gray can be dressed up with vibrant colors such as red, bright pink, or acid green, and made luxurious but cool with silver or chrome.

It is a classic, timeless shade that works well in both traditional and contemporary settings, although since it tends to work best when dressed up with other colors, it is not an ideal choice for a simple country-style room.

Certain depths of gray, especially darker ones, may have connotations of dirt and dust, so this color is best kept away from food preparation and serving areas and kitchen/dining rooms. It is also a color to avoid in cold rooms that don't get much natural light because it will make the space feel cooler and more dungeonlike.

Darker shades of gray can be used to paint a whole wall, which can then be framed with a bright white or even coal black gloss on the baseboard, door, window frames, and any picture frames. A white, pale lavender, or similarly light-colored ceiling along with a light floor covering will help lessen the intensity of the gray and prevent the room from becoming too oppressive.

ABOVE: *Black and white are the parent shades of gray so the three work together well, but a bright contrasting color such as pink, red, or orange will warm any coolness that might exist in a monochromatic scheme.*

RIGHT: *Shades of gray vary from pearly white to darkest charcoal and can be found in many guises, from the matte surfaces of clay pots to the cool feel of polished metal. It can be married with other colors by adding a touch of the contrasting color to the basic gray paint.*

Black can be difficult to live with on all four walls, so darker shades of gray can be used instead. The gray will have a similar weighty appearance but without being quite as solid and negative. At the opposite end of the scale, a gray white is useful because it isn't as strict or strong as a pure white, which can make muted colors look grubby or shabby if used alongside them.

REFERENCE POINTS

To see how powerful gray can be, look at a couple of well-known paintings by the artist James Abbot McNeil Whistler. One of his best-known portraits is formally titled *Arrangement in Black and Gray No. 1,* but is better known as *The Artist's Mother.* The painting, which now hangs in the Musée D'Orsay in Paris, has a midgray background against which the artist's mother is portrayed in profile, sitting in a chair wearing a dark gray dress.

The eye is drawn to the central figure because she is wearing a white bonnet and white cuffs. A white mount around the black-framed picture on the wall also catches the attention. Another study by Whistler, *Arrangement in Gray and Black No. 1*—a portrait of Thomas Carlyle, now at the City Art Gallery and Museum in Glasgow—shows a similarly subtle use of this shade.

Gray can also be formed from specks of black and white together. Think of woolen tweeds or even birds' feathers, and how at a distance they look gray but on close inspection are a mix of black and white. For example, the gray plover's feathers are a mixture of dark and light shades, but when among the silvery shrubs of its native undergrowth, it is hardly distinguishable from its surroundings. Certain marbles and granites also have the gray-white-black mix, which gives the impression of being gray.

LEFT: *Gray provides a contrast to white but is not as dramatic as black. Gray is a soft, restful color that can be used successfully in many schemes, although in a kitchen or bathroom the shade needs to be chosen carefully as it can also be connected with undesirable ideas of dust, grime, and unwashed surfaces.*

CONTEMPORARY FINISHES

Gray is a popular color with contemporary designers. Stone colors are currently fashionable and can be used in Zen-style schemes that are simple and understated. A glass dish or bowl of smooth gray seaside pebbles, either dry or submerged in water to reveal their glistening qualities, is a much-used accessory in modern homes and arrangements.

Other shades that are named after their natural counterparts are also fashionable. For example, slate and charcoal are now found on many paint manufacturers' lists. Slate, the stone from which the paint takes its name, has gone from being an outdoor, utilitarian material to one that has gained a chic reputation indoors.

Slate tiles, both polished and natural, are found on floors in hallways, bathrooms, and kitchens and, in the latter two rooms, also on walls and countertops. Another gray-based substance that has made its way inside is concrete, which can be stained and textured, in a wide range of finishes. In the basic gray mix it is used for floors, walls, and built-in bases for furniture by a number of architects and designers.

Still in the realms of gray are metal surfaces, such as steel, chrome, and silver. These cool reflective surfaces have an affinity with gray and work well with it. The hard matte surface of concentrate used in kitchen and bathroom environments is often offset with sheets of light reflective or stainless steel.

Another finish that has gray overtones is the sun-bleached and weathered wood and shingles of the houses along the coasts of Martha's Vineyard and Nantucket. This wonderfully textured gray surface has a similar feel to driftwood and works well in schemes that have a watery, windswept theme.

OVERLEAF LEFT: *The slate in this bathroom has been left unpolished so that the natural texture and subtle color variations become a feature of the scheme.*

OVERLEAF RIGHT: *These small slate tiles have been arranged in a grid so that their individual grains and patterns are juxtaposed one against the other, creating a random design.*

If it is difficult to get hold of genuine weathered wood, you could try imitating it by having wood sandblasted to exaggerate the grain. The wood can then be painted with a watered-down color that best matches that of driftwood. When applying the paint, brush it in thoroughly so that the grain shows through and pockets of deep color are avoided, keeping the overall effect light and silvery.

Gray can also be very smart and classic. Gray-and-white striped papers and fabrics have a feeling of precise correctness about them, as with the sharp and tailored overtones of a businessman's shirt. If bright colors are set against it, gray can become more relaxed and fun, but still smart.

Fabrics that are best known for being gray are wool flannel and felt, both of which have become fashionable for interior decoration. The brushed textural surfaces of these warm fabrics make them cozy and snug, and manufacturers now produce grades and finishes of these cloths that can be used for upholstery and mats.

For a low-key, log-cabin style, a thick gray rug or throw could be edged with a blanket stitch in brightly colored wool or, for a more urbane and sophisticated setting, with a band of black tape or leather. Softer gray materials include dove gray silk and oyster, mother-of-pearl-like iridescent satin, but these are boudoir fabrics and are best not to be used in general reception rooms.

It can be very tricky using gray in places where white might be expected, such as on bed linen and bath towels. Make sure you choose a shade that is positively and unwaveringly gray, avoiding wishy-washy pale shades that may make it look as though your whites accidentally got washed with a load of darks.

FROM FLOOR LEVEL UP

As a floor covering, gray is very practical. This is especially so with the darker shades because they won't show up the odd mark or scuff, although white threads and pale-colored marks will be visible. Gray is also a common shade for many natural materials used on floors, such as slate, concrete, marble, and flagstone. As a background, gray will frame and accentuate any colorful rugs or mats placed upon it.

Even on a staircase, a decorative bright runner will be complemented by painting the woodwork on either side a shade of gray. If the runner is held in place by stair rods, those made of metal—especially buffed pewter or matte steel—will create an attractive frame.

Gray carpets and tiles can provide grounding to a room decorated in vivid colors or very pale tones, without being too much of a contrast. In a room with pale blue walls, for example, a dark, midnight blue carpet might be too dramatic while a blue gray carpet would be more agreeable.

LIGHTING A GRAY ROOM

The arrangement of lighting in a predominately gray room will be subject to the absorption element of black in the mix. If there is more white than black then the light will be reflected, but if it has a heavier quantity of black in its makeup, more of the light will be absorbed.

Mid- to light shades of gray should be easy to live with during daylight hours, but darker tones may need more lighting. Be choosy about lightbulbs and ensure you don't have too much yellow as this may turn a blue gray background into a sludgy green. Also, avoid too much blue tone in the bulb as this could make a blue gray appear icy.

This predominantly gray kitchen tile wall covering is a mosaic of various shades enlivened with a silver branch-and-leaf motif. Gray and silver have similar base notes so they blend together well, and the silver can counteract the perceived dullness of darker shades of gray.

ABOVE: *Because of their neutral overtones, paler shades of gray and brown can be used together effectively. In this woven horsehair cushion cover a whole gamut of these colors and shades can be seen. The irregular pattern also makes the cover interesting.*

RIGHT: *Being a calm and restful color, gray is ideal for a bedroom, but the overall scheme should be light to avoid the gray becoming dominant and oppressive. If the gray is dark and overpowering, feelings of rest and relaxation may turn to depression and inertia.*

THE SOURCES OF GRAY

Charcoal gray is a color that comes from the burned and charred remains of wood, and the resultant charcoal is used as a drawing material for artists rather than in interior decoration. Gray paint and dye is usually made by blending together white and black. Most early white finishes were not pure: They often contained elements of gray, brown, or blue in their composition, but a white pigment with a lead base was among the most successful and was used by both the Romans and the Chinese.

The lead pigment finishes were followed by **chalk- and lime-based distemper** and **whitewash**, which were used to decorate walls both inside and outside the house. In the 1920s, following the introduction of **titanium oxide**, a brighter and more stable form of white paint evolved.

MOODS OF GRAY

Being surrounded by gray can make you feel secure, but may also exacerbate feelings of depression. It is a tranquil, noncompetitive color but may have links with sadness and melancholy, as well as a lack of direction. If the shade has more white than black in it, the positive aspect of white will offer some redress. White is a color that portrays purity and encourages clear thoughts, although it may endorse feelings of isolation.

Black is a shade rather than a color, and although it may appear to be just one solid dark mass there can be subtle variations, such as blue black, ebony, and anthracite. Black is referred to as a "subtractive" shade because it absorbs light. In fact, it absorbs all the wavelengths that make color, hence it is used for blackout curtains and in cinemas to prevent light from entering or leaving a room.

Although black has many negative associations, being a color linked with death and mourning, it is also a shade of sophistication and elegance. Black-tie evening wear usually involves an elegantly tailored black suit, white shirt, and black bow tie for the man and a long evening dress for the woman, and the height of chic attire is the proverbial little black dress worn for cocktail parties and soirées. Limousines and cars of state and occasion, such as the Rolls Royce and Daimler, are usually black as well.

The surface finish you choose for black will have an important effect on the overall appearance of your scheme. Shiny blacks will reflect a certain amount of light because the surface is reflective, although the color itself is not. So metallic and high-gloss or glazed finishes will create a less oppressive and richer feel. Matte black will appear solid and receding, which is not a good effect to have over a large area of wall or floor.

Other matte surfaces, such as wool, felt, or knitted cotton, will have a similar effect to matte paint, but shiny finishes like silk, satin, and polished leather will have the reflective element. Some pile materials, such as a good quality velvet and fake fur, also have a slight sheen, which enhances the material's richness and texture and gives more visual appeal than the matte surface.

Black was a popular shade in the 1920s, with many textile designs printed on a black background. This was also a time of renewed interest in things oriental, so black lacquer also became popular. Oriental black lacquer boxes, screens, and chairs with mother-of-pearl inlay were part of the era's look, with the black background providing a foil to the delicate iridescent inlay.

The furniture of Eileen Gray, who produced her Nonconformist and "S" chairs in 1926 and 1932, used a combination of chromed tubular metal and black leather upholstery. This marriage of surfaces was popular with many designers and in various areas of interior design. For example, Le Corbusier's Grand Confort chromed bent-steel armchair is finished with black leather cushions; his famous ergonomically sculpted recliner, the B306, which was first produced in 1928, is still most commonly sold with a black leather cover. The Eames' Models 670 and 671 (armchair and footstool) in rosewood-faced, molded plywood are often portrayed and sold with black leather cushions.

COLOR COMBINATIONS

Like purple, black is usually best used as a secondary color, so that rather than painting all four walls with it, you make a feature of a single wall or use black for accessories within the room. An anthracite- (just a note lighter than lamp or coal black) colored sofa or armchair will look dramatic and contemporary against a yellow wall, or scattered with lime green cushions. But make sure there are other black elements in the room, such as a coffee table or leather-covered footstool, so that the sofa is not the only dark object set against lighter and brighter surroundings.

These gloss-finished black walls create a dramatic and complimentary backdrop to the two gilt-framed panels and pair of white porcelain ginger jars. The two chairs have been upholstered in a contrasting, light shade and the baseboard painted in brilliant white to provide a definitive break between the black walls and gray slate floor.

If a black upholstered sofa or chair is large and dominant in a room with a pale scheme and less solid furniture, then scattering a few cushions or a contrasting colored throw over the chair or sofa will make it feel less prominent and bulky within the room.

Black and white are often used together in schemes because they balance each other, the white offering a bright contrast to the darkness of black; together they are the ultimate visual indication of positive and negative. But used alone they can be a stark pair, so it is advisable to introduce a third color. The warmer shades of orange, scarlet, and gold will bring a change of focus and a little relief to such a scheme, but deep purples and blues are not so suitable because they are dark and light-absorbent like black.

Cream is another shade that is often used with black; it is a less dramatic opposite than white and has warm elements in its makeup. Black and cream or ivory are found in dominoes and the keys of a piano. Black wood ebony, a dense hardwood that can be polished to a high gloss, was often worked with ivory in African tribal art. But ivory is now a banned material and can no longer be bought, and even artifacts containing ivory should only be purchased through licensed dealers.

Black can also be mixed with brown, terra-cotta, and pale- or golden-colored wood. In classical times the designs and motifs on urns and vases were often depicted in black against a background of deep terra-cotta. Pale wood and black is representative of the neoclassical period and is seen in Biedermeier furniture; for a more contemporary take on the black-and-brown combination, black wood furniture can look good with tan leather cushions or upholstery.

This monochromatic bathroom is dark but dramatic. The effect is achieved with black mosaic tiles but, because the tiles are small and edged with white grout, the impact of the black is reduced. The white sinks, well-positioned lighting, and large mirror also enhance the feeling of light and space.

PERIOD COLOR SCHEMES

Black can be used to great effect in creating a decadent Art Deco-style bathroom, starting with a black enamel bath and gleaming silver taps and surrounding them with shining black ceramic tiles. Over a square, period-style sink hang a round silver-framed mirror with beveled edges, and the molding could be painted bright pink, the same shade as the carpet.

For a less self-indulgent but still period-style scheme, black can be teamed with white. The tiles can be mainly white but mixed with a border of black to form a checkerboard effect. Or the black tiles could be arranged to make a Charles Rennie Mackintosh-style pattern, in groups of three with the central tile dropped one space below the two on either side. This motif could be repeated in panels in the center of otherwise white walls.

Although quite stark, this V-shaped decorative motif introduces an element of pattern that, in a small room such as a bathroom, will not be too overwhelming. Black can work well in a bathroom, especially if included in shiny ceramic tiles and a gloss paint finish, because light will be reflected from the surface and mirrors, especially a large one over a sink, helping to redress the light balance.

LEFT: *The walls of this room are painted with black wash over a white base. This creates areas where the black is full strength and others where it is diluted, so that overall it appears less dense and solid.*

ABOVE: *Black can be very stylish in a contemporary setting, not only as a paint finish but also in upholstery and curtain fabrics. Many examples of modern classic furniture are covered with black leather.*

LEFT AND ABOVE: *Black-and-white checkerboard patterns are universally popular and timeless. The monochromatic design can be found on walls in kitchens and bathrooms, as well as on floors in most rooms of the house, in conservatories, and in patios. The light and dark contrast is clean and uncomplicated.*

GETTING THE BALANCE RIGHT

Black is sometimes used in kitchens, but it has to be carefully balanced with lighter colors, and when surfaces are shiny, such as tiles on floors or countertops, they must be kept clean and polished as smears and marks will make the place appear messy and unhygienic. The same standards of cleaning should also be used for black tiles in a bathroom.

In a sitting or dining room, a single black painted or fabric-covered wall framed by white or brightly painted woodwork can provide a dramatic backdrop to a collection of artwork. For example, a bright and vividly painted tribal mask, picked out from the background by a halogen spotlight, would make a dramatic tableau. Gilded or silvered objects, such as a group of ornately framed small mirrors, would sparkle against black; framed black-and-white photographs also work well on a black background. Precise linear architectural drawings are another effective option.

A panel of black behind a console table or sideboard also works well because the table in effect reduces the amount of blackness on show. On top of the table an array of objects could be displayed, such as fine white porcelain vases and bowls, with perhaps a few red rosy apples or red rose petals in one of the bowls for a splash of color.

Black and white can be a sophisticated combination, but the quantities of each color should be balanced. The outer canopy of this bed is black but the lining is white. The curtains at the windows are black but are balanced by white blinds and a sharp white border on the pelmet. The walls are black but the floor is white, so the ratio of each shade is equal.

IRONWORK

One decorative feature that is often used in furniture, balustrades, and other decorative embellishments in the home is wrought ironwork. It is frequently found in period houses, especially in Regency and Victorian buildings. This hard-wearing and durable iron in curled and twisted metalwork is often painted black.

Wrought-iron furniture is frequently finished with a durable gloss paint, especially if it is the sort of furniture that lives in a conservatory or makes its way out onto a patio or garden during the summer. But metalwork indoors can be made even more impressive if painted in a softer satin finish with a slight sheen. Furniture and balustrades painted in this way will look elegant and especially attractive in a hallway or stairwell where the walls are painted in a pale color, such as pink or a rich cream. The furls and tendrils of the ironwork will stand out clearly and decoratively against the pale walls.

FLOORS AND FABRICS

When it comes to flooring, black is most often teamed with white. Traditional black-and-white checkerboard flooring can be created many different ways and is suitable for almost every room, from the conservatory and kitchen to the hall and bathroom. The checks can be made from marble, linoleum, or ceramic tiles, or can simply be painted by squaring off the floor, masking in areas with tape, and then painting, as explained on page 151.

Wooden flooring that is past its prime or is made from cheaper planks can be easily made to look smart with a couple coats of black gloss paint.

As black is a very dense color it may take a few coats of paint to build up an even and deep cover.

Black carpeting is rarely used because although it won't show black marks it will show everything else, from dust and white threads to colored specks and even mud particles that may be stuck in the treads on the soles of your shoes. However, if you are attracted to the idea of a black floor, make sure that it is in a finish that can be easily cleaned and in a room where there is little heavy traffic.

When it comes to fabrics, there are many that feature black, although apart from blackout fabric it is a color that almost never appears on its own. Among the most dramatic of the black-and-white fabrics available is a good regular stripe; it looks clean, fresh, and dramatic, highly reminiscent of Cecil Beaton's striking costumes for Audrey Hepburn in the film *My Fair Lady*.

Black can also be teamed with other colors in striped fabrics, as well as zanier geometric designs such as checkerboard, zigzags, and polka dots. A band of plain black material, broad tape, or ribbon can also be used as edging to create a border around curtains or blinds. The edge will define the limits and make a frame for the main material inside.

Another textile design that is seen in just black and white is by the London-based firm Timney Fowler. Their profile of a classic Roman head printed in repeats in black on a white background received international acclaim. It is a simple combination but has been used to create a powerful and appealing image.

In some settings a minimal amount of furnishings and patterns will create maximum impact. In this neutral scheme the black-and-white upholstered chairs look vivid and eye-catching. The black painted legs of the chairs contrast with the sleek silvered legs of the table, and the black frame of the painting above complements the linear stripe in the fabric.

Lighting black

As explained before, black is an absorbent color; there is not much point in trying to light a matte black surface as it will have little effect. A shiny surface will be responsive, but it is often better to concentrate lighting on the objects or furniture that are set against the black background.

While it is always a good idea to have side or table lights beside armchairs or at either end of a sofa, it is even more important in the case of black upholstery because there will be little or no light reflected from the surface of the furniture. An adjustable light may be especially beneficial as the beam can be accurately focused on a book or newspaper. If the furniture is black and chrome, focus the lights carefully or you may find that a harsh glare occurs when the beam reflects off the metal.

ABOVE: *Metal finishes such as steel, chrome, and aluminum will create a contemporary feel and contrast well with black and white. These conical sinks and disc-style mirrors stand out against the dark supporting wall.*

LEFT: *Black-and-white printed fabrics are a good way to bring a bold pattern into a scheme. Here, the profile of a Roman emperor's head is printed in white on a black background. This positive-negative combination can also be seen in the upholstery fabric on the chair and the stripe of the tablecloth, the diverse patterns working well together because of their common coloring.*

THE SOURCES OF BLACK

*For many years **lampblack** was used as a black pigment in inks and paints. Lampblack is made by burning liquid hydrocarbons, such as kerosene, with an insufficient quantity of air, which produces a smoky flame. The smoke or soot is collected and used as the coloring agent. Now, **carbon black** is more commonly used. It is composed of finer particles and is sometimes referred to as "gas black" because it is produced by incomplete combustion of natural gas.*

*Natural black dyestuff was obtained from **squid**, which releases an inky black substance when in danger. The cloud of black creates a shield or screen, which allows the squid time to escape from its assailant.*

MOODS OF BLACK

Black is associated with the element of water. It can be a source of inspiration as it provides a blank point on which to focus, but in large quantities can be oppressive. In heraldic terms, black is used to denote prudence, wisdom, and constancy. In churches, it is the color of funerals and is usually thought of as a mortuary color denoting grief, despair, and death, although some churches use purple instead. Black represents the metal lead, the precious stone diamond, and the planet Saturn.

List of Suppliers

PAINTS

Behr

Tel: 800-854-0133

Web: www.behrpaint.com

Benjamin Moore & Co.

Tel: 800-826-2623

Web: www.benjaminmoore.com

Farrow & Ball

Tel: 877-363-1040

Web: www.farrow-ball.com

*Makers of the National Trust range of paints,
including Picture Gallery Red and Eating Room Red*

Fine Paints of Europe

Tel: 800-332-1556

Web: www.fine-paints.com

*Also carries Martha Stewart Living Color
Collections*

The Glidden Company

Tel: 800-221-4100

Web: www.gliddenpaint.com

Janovic Plaza

Tel: 800-772-4381

Web: www.janovic.com

Martin Senour Paints

Tel: 800-MSP-5270

Web: www.martinsenour.com

Pittsburgh Paints

Tel: 800-441-9695

Web: www.pittsburghpaints.com

Pratt & Lambert

Tel: 800-BUY-PRAT

Web: www.prattandlambert.com

Ralph Lauren

Tel: 800-783-4586

Web: www.paintplus.com

The Sherwin Williams Company

Tel: 800-4-SHERWIN

Web: www.sherwinwilliams.com

Waverly Waterborne Interior Finish

Tel: 800-631-3440

Web: www.decoratewaverly.com

GENERAL HOME DECOR

ABC Carpet & Home

Tel: 212-473-3000

Web: www.abccarpet.com

*Furniture, accessories, bedding, table linens,
lighting, fabric, rugs*

Crate & Barrel

Tel: 800-967-6696

Web: www.crateandbarrel.com

Furniture, accessories, bedding, table linens, curtains

Domain

Tel: 800-436-6246

Web: www.domain-home.com

Furniture, accessories

Dragonfly Designs

Tel: 800-711-9111

Web: www.dragonflytenbest.com

Furniture; huge selection of fabric grouped by color

GoodHome.com

Tel: 877-642-2487

Web: www.goodhome.com

Fabrics, furniture, accessories

HomePortfolio Inc.

Tel: 800-840-0118

Web: www.homeportfolio.com

Furniture, accessories, bedding, table linens, curtains, lighting; also paints

Latimer Alexander

Tel: 800-654-2313

Web: latimeralexander.com

Velvets, chenilles

Mitchell Gold Co.

Tel: 800-789-5401

Web: www.mitchellgold.com

Furniture, slipcovers

Modern Home

Web: www.modernhome.com

Furniture, accessories

Palazzetti

Tel: 888-881-1199

Web: www.palazzetti.com

Furniture, lighting, rugs

Pottery Barn

Tel: 888-779-5176

Web: www.potterybarn.com

Furniture, accessories, bedding, table linens, slipcovers, curtains

Salvage One

Tel: 312-733-0098

Web: www.salvageone.com

Furniture, lighting, architectural elements

Silk Trading Co.

Tel: 800-854-0396

Web: www.silktrading.com

Fabrics; draperies; milk-based paints resembling 18th-century casein paints

StyleForLiving

Tel: 323-467-8918

Web: www.styleforliving.com

Furniture, accessories, bedding, lighting, fabric

Uncommon Goods

Tel: 888-365-0056

Web: www.uncommongoods.com

Accessories, bedding, lighting

Acknowledgments

The publisher would like to thank the following photographers and agencies for their kind permission to reproduce their pictures in this book.

2–3 James Mortimer/Interior Archive (Artist: David Carter); 4–5 Cecilia Innes/Interior Archive (Artist: Erik Bendsten); 8–9 Ray Main/Mainstream; 10 Tatyana Hill Jan Baldwin/Narratives; 12–13 Simon Brown/Interior Archive (Designer: Christophe Gollut); 13 right Christian Sarramon (Alan Faena, Buenos Aires); 14–15 David Churchill/Arcaid (Architect: D. Churchill and P. Vafadari); 16 left Henry Wilson/Interior Archive (Architect: Charles Rutherfoord); 16–17 Ray Main/Mainstream; 18 Tatyana Hill Jan Baldwin/Narratives; 19 Solvi dos Santos; 20 © Verne (Design: Manu Demuynck); 21 Timney Fowler—The Aesthetic Collection; 22–3 Christian Sarramon (Alan Faena, Buenos Aires); 24 Ray Main/Mainstream; 25 Tatyana Hill Jan Baldwin/Narratives; 27 Christopher Simon-Sykes/Interior Archive (Ragley Hall/Great Houses of England & Wales); 28–9 English Heritage P. L.; 30–1 Simon Upton/Interior Archive (Owner: Lisa St. Aubin de Teran); 34–5 Solvi dos Santos; 37 Tim Beddow/Interior Archive (Artist: Beazy Bailey); 38–9 Urban Research Laboratory/Photograph: Michael Mack; 39 right Jean-Francois Jaussaud; 40 left Simon Upton/Interior Archive (Owner: Lisa St. Aubin de Teran); 40–1 James Mortimer/Interior Archive (Property: Leighton House); 42 Robert Harding Syndication/Inspirations/Gloria Nicol; 44–5 Solvi dos Santos; 45 right Ray Main/Mainstream; 46 Christian Sarramon (La Lunita/Cahen d'Anvers); 47 Solvi dos Santos; 48–9 Nicholas Kane/Arcaid (Architect: Niall McLaughlin); 50 Nicholaas Maritz Jan Baldwin/Narratives; 51 Deidi von Schaewen; 52–53 James Mortimer/Interior Archive (Artist: David Carter); 53 right Solvi dos Santos; 55 James Mortimer/Interior Archive (Artist: David Carter); 56 left Solvi dos Santos; 56 right Tim Clinch/Interior Archive; 57 left Jan Baldwin/Narratives; 57–9 Solvi dos Santos; 60 Debi Treloar/www.elizabethwhiting.com; 61 right © M.Angelo/Corbis; 62–3 Fritz von der Schulenburg/Interior Archive (Designer: Jenny Hall); 64 Simon Kenny/Belle/Arcaid (Architect: Ian Stapleton); 65 Christian Sarramon (Alan Faena, Buenos Aires); 66 Paul Ryan/International Interiors (Designer: Kathy Gallagher); 67 Tim Beddow/Interior Archive; 69 Mary Shaw Patrick van Robaeys/Narratives; 70 Fritz von der Schulenburg/Interior Archive (Designer: Anouska Hempel); 71 www.elizabethwhiting.com; 73 Ray Main/Mainstream; 74 Andrew Wood/Interior Archive (Artist: Arabella Johnsen); 75 Fair Lady/Camera Press; 77 Paul Ryan/International Interiors (Architect: Fell-Clark Design); 78 Ray Main/Mainstream; 80 Solvi dos Santos; 81 Gross & Daley (Morgan Puett); 83 above © Kevin Schafer/Corbis; 83 below Solvi dos Santos; 84 Photonica/Ryu; 86–7 Ray Main/Mainstream/Ozwald Boateng; 88 Mary Shaw Patrick van Robaeys/Narratives; 89 Inside/Interior Archive/House & Leisure/G.McAllister; 90 left Jan Baldwin/Narratives; 90–1 IPC Syndication/Homes & Gardens/James Merrell; 92–3 Deidi von Schaewen; 94–5 Ray Main/Mainstream/Designer: Roger Oates; 95 right Deidi von Schaewen; 96 Fritz von der Schulenburg/Interior Archive (Property: Blakes); 97 Tim Clinch/Interior Archive (Property: Madrid); 98 Edina van der Wyck/Interior Archive (Designer: Jenny Armit); 99 © Verne (Architect: Raymond Jacquemijns); 100 Ray Main/Mainstream; 101 Tim Clinch/Interior Archive (Property: Madrid); 102 Ted Yarwood (Rebecca Last Interiors, Toronto); 103 Deidi von Schaewen; 104 Andreas von Einsiedel/www.elizabethwhiting.com; 105 Tom Leighton/www.elizabethwhiting.com; 106 Paul Ryan/International Interiors (Designer: Wolfgang Joop); 108 Eric Morin/Interior Archive; 109 Solvi dos Santos; 110–1 Jacques Dirand/Interior Archive (Designer: Michel Klein); 113 above left Tim Beddow/Interior Archive; 113 above right Max Jourdan/Camera Press; 113 below Solvi dos Santos; 114 Ray Main/Mainstream/Ozwald Boateng; 116–7 Verne/Houses & Interiors; 118 Jonathan Pilkington/Interior Archive (Designer: Hamish Bowles); 119 Brian Harrison/Red Cover (Muralist: Alan Dodd); 121 Simon Upton/Interior Archive (Designer: Carol Thomas); 122 SHE/Camera Press; 123 David Loftus; 124 IPC Syndication/Homes & Gardens/David George; 125 Tim Beddow/Interior Archive (Designer: Rana Kabbani); 126 left Ray Main/Mainstream; 126–7 Ray Main/Mainstream; 127 right Ray Main/Mainstream; 128 Andrew Wood/Interior Archive (Owner: Mandy Coakley); 129 Mirjam Bleeker/Taverne Agency and Frank Visser; 130–1 IPC Syndication/Homes & Gardens/Thomas Stewart; 132 above © Michelle Garrett/Corbis; 132 below © Ralph A. Clevenger/Corbis; 134 left Ted Yarwood; 134–5 Tim Imrie/www.elizabethwhiting.com; 136 Sarie Visi/Camera Press; 137 Ted Yarwood (Brian Gluckstein Design Planning, Toronto); 138 Sarie Visi/Camera Press; 139 Laura Ellenberger/Camera Press; 140 Solvi dos Santos; 141 Polly Farquharson (J. Rutherford-Best); 142–3 Deidi von Schaewen; 143 right Fernando Bengoechea/Interior Archive (Owner: Sarofim); 144 Ted Yarwood (Powell & Bonneil Design Consultants, Toronto); 145 Gross & Daley (Richard Warholic); 146 Henry Wilson/Interior Archive (Designer: Ivan Speight); 149 Ray Main/Mainstream; 150 IPC Syndication/Homes & Gardens/Thomas Stewart; 152 left Solvi dos Santos; 152–3 www.elizabethwhiting.com; 153 Polly Farquharson (Antoni & Alison); 154–5 Mads Mogensen; 156 Rodney Hyett/ www.elizabethwhiting.com; 157 Fernando Bengoechea/Interior Archive (Owner: Sharone Einhorn); 158 Paul Ryan/International Interiors (Designer: Sharone Einhorn); 160 Christian Sarramon; 161 Polly Farquharson (*Elle Deco*); 162 Inside/Interior Archive/Maison Française/N.Tosi; 164 left Peter Ting Jan Baldwin/Narratives (David Champion); 164–5 Brian Harrison/Red Cover (Paolo Moschino); 166 Jan Baldwin/Narratives; 167 Tim Street-Porter/www.elizabethwhiting.com; 168 Christian Sarramon; 169 © Verne (Architect: Nathalie Van Reeth); 170 IPC Syndication/Homes & Gardens/Simon Upton; 172–3 © Verne (Designer: Manu Demuynck); 174 Victor Watts/Houses & Interiors; 175 Ray Main/Mainstream/Architect: Sablha Foster; 176–7 Christian Sarramon; 177 right David Champion Jan Baldwin/Narratives; 178–9 Fritz von der Schulenburg/Interior Archive (Property: Blakes); 180 Richard Felber; 182 Timney Fowler—Neoclassical Collection; 183 Fair Lady/Camera Press; Christain Sarramon; 185 Jan Baldwin/Narratives.